Service Management Made Simple

Automotive Aftermarket Training, Inc.

Automotive Aftermarket Training, Inc. designs and delivers training curriculum for the automotive industry. Automotive Aftermarket Training was founded by OE Manufacturer industry experts who specialize in technical training, troubleshooting, service management practices and customer retention. The curriculum at AAT is designed and developed by these same industry experts. AAT provides repair shops, and automotive related companies, of all sizes, with training seminars, hands-on training programs, and business growth consulting services aimed at growing customer satisfaction, improving customer retention, and increasing car count.

Table of Contents

Introduction

The Third Edition of this book incorporates lessons learned since the two publications, additions that seemed more important in today's business climate than maybe they had when the book was first written, and a focus on business practices for those who own their own repair shops, or soon will. It continues to be heavy on customer satisfaction as this seems to be an area that is ripe with potential, improving customer retention (which has taken a hit with the average number of customer visits being greatly reduced these days), and making service management less frustrating and more effective. This edition includes best practices in marketing, employee management and business growth for those who have begun a successful venture in automotive repair, but who may be wondering why they cannot seem to get further ahead.

Two companion workbooks The Toolbox, and the Automotive Shop Owner's Daily Business Planner was also written as a way to help shop owners and managers organize their thoughts, implement marketing programs, and keep track of things their electronic systems don't allow them to.

Since the last edition, the automotive service industry has survived and thrived during the Covid Pandemic. During a time when vehicle owners should have reduced the number of miles driven, the industry rediscovered just how really important automobiles are to people. Not only were car counts up, but people were pumping money into their used automobiles as they couldn't get new ones due to supply chain issues. Eventually the spare parts supply chain tripped up, and we found parts harder to come by, but that didn't stop customers from wanting work done. It was yet another reminder that being in the automotive service industry can provide job security and financial stability.

Even with good times galore, running an automotive repair shop, or even working in an automotive service operation is continually challenging. No matter what the economy does, where technology takes us, or however hard it is to find quality employees, there will be vehicles on the road that need repair for a very long time still. Yes, electric vehicles are on their way, and time will tell how the industry will change, but for now you can expect things to stay good for a while.

The key to surviving the many challenges found in our business is of course the customer. Customers are the reason any of us have a job. They can make our jobs feel very rewarding, or make us wish we had made a different career choice when we'd had the chance. Knowing how to handle your customers, learning to understand their expectations, and working to create a positive experience for every customer will make your job easier and more enjoyable, and it will help you become more profitable.

Being able to retain customers once they've come to you steadies revenue, reduces advertising and marketing costs, and helps build a positive reputation. I will likely always maintain that t*he key to customer retention is customer satisfaction.* Customer satisfaction is arrived at through an understanding of who your customer is, by hiring the right employees (and providing them with the appropriate training), and always utilizing effective, consistent processes throughout your organization.

Owning, or operating a service repair facility certainly can be overwhelming at times, especially when things get busy. It's easy to fall back on old habits and ways of coping. Dealing with customers, managing employees, fixing cars, and making sure the business is profitable can be a tough job. Doing what needs to be done to grow your business may seem much easier thought of than executed. Operating a profitable, successful automotive repair facility doesn't have to be complicated though. I continue to be a proponent of keeping things simple – especially during these times of increasing complexity. Anchor yourself in KISS (Keep It Simple Silly) and you will find your way successfully through most any challenge.

There are simple and easy things that you can do to help improve the customer and employee experience while growing business. In the following pages you will find what 35 years of automotive experience have taught me about running a service facility. I don't claim to be the world's foremost expert on automotive service management. In my opinion, nobody ever will be. However, I can deliver to you what myself, and many others, have done to run business more productively, with higher gross profit, and less turmoil and do so in a way that will help you to meet and exceed your business goals.

In writing this book, I've tried to make it as easy as possible to identify key nuggets of information that can make a difference in managing your service facility. Best practices, key ideas, and useful resources have all been called out and highlighted for easy recognition and reference. If you don't want to read the book cover to cover, then just pick it up once each day and flip it open to a callout box to pick up a tidbit that you can build on today.

In the appendix you will find information useful in the everyday operation of your facility. Customer problem analysis sheets, work schedule examples, financial statement examples, and lists of resources can be found there. You can also find training videos on YouTube at **GregMarchandRepairShopRescueCoach** that support the content found in this book. The videos are short, concise, and intended to reinforce and further explain the content written about here.

I encourage the reader to share this book with service writers, technicians, or other employees who can gain from understanding the overall operational goals of an automotive service facility. Everyone working together makes the biggest difference in the success of an organization. Use the thought starters the end of the book to think about where you might be able to take your business, and what the first steps might be.

As with any venture, successful service management is an evolving process. Customers change, cultures change, demographics change, and employee expectations change. Take what you can from this book, and combine it with your own experience, your own market, and those processes you have found to work well for you. And lastly, *never* stop learning and growing!

Chapter 1: Customers

> ## In This Chapter
>
> - **What the customer means to your shop.**
> - **How customers view the service experience.**
> - **Types of customers.**
> - **What customers want.**

What the customer means to you

Customers mean everything to your business. Without the money they spend with you to maintain and repair their vehicle, you wouldn't be in business. A single customer can represent a significant amount of money to your repair shop. Happy customers bring other customers, make going to work every day more fulfilling, and reduce advertising and marketing expense. Unhappy customers will do the exact opposite. Unhappy customers can quickly tarnish the reputation of a repair facility, make going to work painful, and force you to spend more in advertising to continually conquest a replacement customer. Unfortunately, it seems easy to forget just what the customer means to an automotive repair facility in terms of organizational sustainability.

Understanding what motivates your customer and seeing the service experience through your customer's eyes is critical to establishing high levels of customer satisfaction. High customer satisfaction levels lead to high customer retention, and high customer retention means more gross profit.

Key Point

Customer Lifetime Value (CLV) can be as much as $200,000 today. Work to earn their business!

There are various dollar figures associated with what the average customer spends on service and maintenance over the course of their lifetime. Some studies have suggested each customer is worth $200,000 to an individual repair shop over the period of their lifetime, while other studies have suggested numbers higher and lower than this. Whichever number you choose to associate with each customer, the bottom line is that your customers are worth a lot of money to you. Without customers, we aren't in business. Without regular customers, those customers that return to us again and again, the job of managing a service facility profitably becomes far more difficult. Many repair shops can stay in business with the number of customers they have, but they will continue to struggle when trying to grow the business. Happy customers bring more customers – always!

Customers beget customers. A friend of mine often told me "there are three people in your life that you need to trust…your doctor, your hairdresser, and your mechanic". Many people feel this way and as such, word of mouth is trusted when someone goes looking for a new mechanic or repair shop. By providing your customers the best service experience possible, you can help ensure free advertising to potential customers that you might never otherwise have access to. Remember, most people will ask friends and family who they should have service their automobile.

Key Point

With a few screen touches, customers can spread negative word about your business across your market in only a few seconds. This alone makes it important that every effort is made to communicate well, gather information well, and satisfy each customer.

Of course, the flip side of the customer experience is seen in the old adage "a happy customer tells one person, while an unhappy customer tells 10 people". This "negative" advertising can hurt your business without you even knowing it. Have you ever driven past a restaurant and thought "I've always wanted to try that place, but so-and-so says it was horrible"?

Often just the word of a trusted friend, positive or negative, is enough to influence a customer's purchase decision.

Today, the word of a stranger in your social network has the same effect. Even happy customers always seem to be looking for a new repair shop these days. Loyalty is thin, if not non-existent. Seeing a negative review written about an experience on Google or Reddit is enough to ensure a potential new customer is never known to you. The same is true of the customers that visit your repair facility – one poor experience and they may just disappear without another word said.

One of the major problems with unhappy customers is the fact that you may not know they left your shop unhappy. They pay their invoice, walk out, and never return. This is a problem not only because you just lost a customer, but because you never had the opportunity to fix what the customer was upset about. Not being able to fix something that upset one customer may mean the action that created one unhappy customer will continue and cause you to lose more customers in the same manner. This is a case where what you don't know *will* hurt you. That first $200,000 you lost could quickly turn into $1 million in lost revenue – within days. The worst part may be that you never even knew it.

Depending on how you keep track of customers at your automotive repair facility, whether it's with written records, or management software, it is extremely difficult to track lost customers. *Losing a customer can be bad enough, not knowing how you lost the customer is far worse.* Paying close attention to each detail of the service process is the best way to safeguard against losing a disgruntled customer over something small. We will discuss the service process in detail later in the book. For now, let's take a closer look at the customer.

Good Customer vs Bad Customer

In discussing what constitutes a good customer versus a bad customer, I'm not trying to paint the picture that all customers are wonderful to work with. I only ask you to remember that each and every customer is worth a lot of money to your repair facility. When I ask someone in a service facility to describe a good customer, I get answers that range from "ones that spend tons of money" to "someone who brings us donuts every week". In general, many in the industry consider a good customer to be one who brings their vehicle in regularly, doesn't question the bill, doesn't take up too much of our time, and doesn't ask too many questions. If this is what represents a good customer to you, that's fine, but defining a "good" customer in this manner leaves out any customer that doesn't already behave in this manner.

I prefer to define a "good customer" as one who has a positive service experience every time they come to the shop. Why? To me, this is a good customer because I know they will consistently spend money with the shop over a long period of time and will likely provide positive word-of-mouth advertising among their family and friends. A positive customer experience means they'll be less anxious about having their vehicle worked on and will be more likely to visit the shop for regular maintenance. It also means that any customer referral program I implement in my service operation is likely to be effective.

When asked about what makes for a "bad" customer, the definitions run the gamut from "they never spend any money" to "they always question the bill". I'm not sure this is a good way to define a "bad customer". Is there a "bad" customer? I might suggest that there is no such thing as a bad customer.

Certainly, there are customers that take up an inordinate amount of our time, always seem to have questions upon questions, and sometimes want to watch the work being performed. But are these people really "bad" customers? Do they ever turn into "good customers"? They do.

Key Point

A good customer is one that has a great service experience every time they visit your repair shop.

I also believe that these folks sometimes become some of our best customers. If we're busy, or feeling hassled, it can be tempting to brush these people off and label them as "bad" customers. The next time you find yourself doing this, take a moment to remind yourself what that customer means to you in terms of long-term revenue. Every customer that spends money with your service facility is a "good customer". Each

---

Customer Satisfaction Point

Customers don't generally feel good about having to bring their vehicle into service at an auto repair facility. Anything you can do to make it a pleasant experience for them will go a *long* way!

---

customer that spends money with you has the potential to return again and again and again. Even the challenging customers represent significant revenue potential to your repair facility. Never forget, and ensure that your employees never forget, what each and every customer is worth to your place of business.

To ensure customers return your service facility again and again let's consider what the customer experience might be like from their perspective.

The Customer Experience

If you've been in the automotive business for a long time there are probably many things that you take for granted. The automotive repair shop is where you go to work every day. All of the noises, chaos, things that can go wrong, and diagnostic challenges are familiar to you. At the very least the shop is an environment that you know and understand. This isn't true for your customers.

Many customers show up at your door expecting a less than positive experience when they walk into your repair shop. Why? Many customers aren't comfortable in a repair shop environment. They may have had a previous experience with your shop, or a competitor's shop, in which they walked away feeling like they didn't get all the answers, the repair wasn't properly performed, or they felt that they were treated poorly. They may have been told that they were going to get "ripped off" when they bring their car in for service. They may have bought into the narrative that the automotive industry is dishonest. They also value their vehicle highly, and are often wary of letting someone else drive it, operate it, or do work on it.

Let's face it, many customers feel like they are about to be taken advantage of when they walk through the door. The automotive repair industry doesn't have the best reputation among consumers. Some customers hate paying money for something that has little tangible reward for them, while others dislike the hassle associated with having their vehicle worked on.

In general, service customers act the way that they do out of fear, anxiety, preconceived expectations, or previous experience. Learning to view the customer experience as if you were the one having your vehicle worked on can help to create a better service experience for each of your customers.

Something to Consider

Customers usually act the way they do because they are on the defensive as soon as they walk through the door. No matter what – act like you're glad to see them!

The Customer's Vehicle

Our vehicles are unique to each of us and can be a very personal item in our lives. You may have been in the automotive industry long enough to feel like it's "just another car", but think about what giving your personal car or truck to a stranger to drive, take apart, or repair might be like. It's probably a bit disconcerting isn't it? Have you ever had one of your employees do some work on your vehicle and find that it didn't meet your expectations? You weren't very happy about the situation, were you?

Now pretend that you don't know anything about how a car works, what's involved in replacing a timing belt, or what might be causing an oil leak from your engine. It might be like going to the doctor for you. You know something is wrong, but you must trust someone else to tell you what the problem is, make the correct diagnosis, and fix it properly!

Add to the experience walking into a place of business that has a bunch of strange equipment behind a concrete wall (equipment that you may or may not be able to see), where there's lots of banging, hissing, zipping of air tools, and probably some cussing going on. I liken this experience to walking past the haunted house ride at an amusement park and hearing weird noises and screams. Not really knowing what's going on can make you feel very anxious about what's about to take place. You can imagine the customer's anxiety level increasing with the more they hear, see, or smell. They are often very uncomfortable by the time you are about to greet them.

Something to Consider

I sometimes liken the customer walking into an auto repair shop to the experience of R2D2 and C3PO walking past the robot torture chamber in the original Star Wars movie! There are lots of scary, unusual noises coming out of that shop!

Now we have a customer who is anxious about turning over something that is very personal to them to someone that they may, or may not, know. They don't have any knowledge of what might be wrong, or even of how the vehicle works, and as such, have to trust someone who is a total stranger to tell them the truth about their vehicle's problem. Their prized possession is going to be taken behind a concrete wall into a loud, often dirty, unknown world by a stranger, and they are expected to sit and wait patiently.

Further compounding the experience is the fact that often times the person they are interfacing with is busy, feeling hassled, or is just plain grumpy. The demeanor of the person with whom they are interacting influences how the customer deals with their own anxiety. The attitude of the service writer can either compound the anxiety the customer is already feeling, or help to reduce it. Often, the service writer has no idea the message they are sending with the look on their face, lack of eye contact, or tone of voice.

Key Point

A smile and pleasant greeting can set the tone of a positive service experience!

Remember, customers feel anxious primarily because of what they don't know or don't understand. When a customer is acting grumpy, or aggressive, it's often because of insecurities. Set the tone of the experience for the customer; don't let them set it for you.

Eventually the customer is going to have to pay a whole lot of money for some sort of repair, or service. After they pay the bill, they walk outside, find their vehicle (sometimes easier said than done), get in it.....and most of the time can't see what they just bought. The car feels the same, sounds the same, and looks the same (except for maybe that greasy hand print that wasn't there before).

If you go down to the big box store and purchase a brand-new television, you can come home, plug it in, and see what your $1000 just bought you. Spend that same $1000 on a service, maintenance item, or repair, and what do you get to experience? More times than not...nothing! In a society that relishes gratification of all sorts, this part of the experience leaves a customer feeling less than satisfied.

We are all customers of someone. Whether you're buying pizza, gasoline, boots, or have a bank account, you have a customer experience every day. Think about what makes for a positive customer experience for you. Is it convenience? Is it paying less for something if you buy it somewhere else? Is it the customer service you receive? Or maybe it's just that the representative always seems happy to see you?

Key Point

Customers often can't see, feel, or hear what they've just purchased from you. In today's world of instant gratification, they need some justification for having spent so much money.

In general, customers often have negative expectations when they walk through your door to have their vehicle worked on. Understanding that the customer is not expecting a good experience, and putting measures in place to help your repair shop ensure a good experience for your customer will lead to a customer for life. Managing customer expectations is the job of every employee in your facility.

Trust

When I'm asked what the single most important factor is in getting customers to not only visit a shop, but spend money on repairs and maintenance, my answer is *trust*.

If you were to ask a group of automotive service professionals how many of them had customers who walked in the door,
tossed the keys on the counter and walked away saying "give
me a call when it's done" you would not only get most of
them nodding their heads, but almost every individual asked
will be smiling. They are smiling because everyone loves this
kind of customer.

You see, the factor that allows a customer to behave this way,
is the same factor that causes the customer to say 'yes' when
asked if they'd like to have a brake inspection performed
while the vehicle is here today, or if you can go ahead and get
those parts ordered and installed so that they are not further
inconvenienced. That factor is *trust*.

Creating trust with a customer not only makes them want to
talk about your shop (word-of-mouth advertising), but increases your average repair order dollars and hours, grows
your gross profit, and makes everyone's day a lot better. Selling gets easier, workflow goes more smoothly, and conversations are more pleasant.

How then, can we consistently build more trust with more customers? I suggest that there are two main components to building more trust, with more customers, more consistently: create an Exceptional Customer Service experience, and ensure Fixed Right the First Time.

Building the Customer Satisfaction Pyramid

There are many stories of organizations, and sometimes entire industries, that have struggled to get positive customer feedback to the levels that they expect. Often, especially in the case of health care and automotive service, this is due to not recognizing the importance of the customer experience. When our mindset is on "we fix cars" it gets easy to think that if we diagnose and repair, everyone should be happy.

We then spend a ton of money marketing because we know how well we fix cars, how few comebacks we have, yet still "we just don't have enough customers". Instead of asking how car count can be increased, shop owners and managers should instead be asking "how do we get more customers to trust us?"

When you look that the Customer Satisfaction Pyramid on the previous page you notice that a pyramid could be built just with "Fixed Right First Time", but for how many customers would that hold true?

Ask yourself "if I were the customer, would I be happy if my vehicle were always repaired properly, but it was a pain to get an appointment, the service consultant was always busy and grumpy, and they never charged me the same as what they said they would?"

The answer for most of us is a resounding "No". Having a proper repair or maintenance performed is almost never enough for us. We want the experience, and the product. Not having a great experience may not keep us from going back (as we know at least the car gets fixed), but will we be more likely to try out a different shop next time? Maybe.

Can some customers be happy with just Fixed Right the First Time? They can be...but they represent a very small portion of our overall customer base. Therefore, you must pay attention to building an Exceptional Customer Service Experience, and then adding to it Fixed Right the First Time to get as many customers to *Trust* as you can!

An Exceptional Customer Service Experience does not mean that you must have the comfiest recliners in the waiting room, the biggest television, or even the best coffee in town. Most of the time it just means you must understand your customer at a very basic level, and ensure that you meet that customer's expectations.

If this sounds complicated, it's not. It is more complex than just treating every customer the same though. When you treat every customer the same, you miss what makes a service experience exceptional to each individual.

If you want to create an Exceptional Customer Service Experience, with the end goal being to generate trust, you must understand what motivates each type of customer. That knowledge and understanding must then be combined with service counter process, sales process, and excellent communication skills. Together, these elements will create and keep customer trust, allowing your organization to grow consistently and efficiently.

Visit YouTube: Greg Marchand – Repair Shop Rescue Coach for short training videos that address the creation of trust with your customers, as well as other factors not addressed in this text that influence the level of trust a customer has with you and your repair shop.

Chapter 2 will address the Service Experience and related concepts and processes in more detail, while Chapter 3 will address the key element of Fixed Right First Time. First though, you must understand the Types of Customers.

Types of Customers

As with all things human, customers come in all sorts of designs. Many industry consultants and sociologists group customers in four categories.

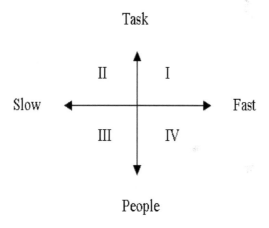

Customers can fall anywhere along the X or Y axis of the above diagram. The important thing to remember is that customers can prefer any combination of fast/slow and task/people oriented transactions. They may prefer quick transactions, or slower transactions, while at the same time they may either prefer things explained to them in detail, or would rather just take your word for what the problem is and how you resolved it. Every customer, just like every person (they are people after all), is different.

Customers that like slower transactions and have a need to understand exactly what went wrong, how it's going to be repaired, and need to understand all of the expenses involved (Quadrant III) may be a challenge to deal with, but are likely to become extremely loyal customers if properly handled. Take time with these customers, explain repairs, and explain their bill in detail they are likely to become some of your very best customers! It may take time and patience, but it will pay off in the end.

Customers who are very task oriented and prefer fast transactions while asking few questions (Quadrant I) may not be your most loyal customers, but are often labeled "good" customers because they are perceived as easy to deal with. In fact, these customers may not be very good customers at all!

Customer Satisfaction Point

Learn to recognize what type of transaction the customer in front of you needs. This is not a tool to be used for stereotyping customers, but a tool to be used to decide "what does this customer, at this point in time, standing before me, need in a transaction?"

Don't confuse Quadrant I customers with the previously mentioned customers who someone spent the necessary time with over the years to build a relationship. It could be that the trust level has been built to a point where the once "difficult" customer is now a "good" customer.

No matter how you define a good customer or a bad customer, remember that each customer behaves the way they do for a reason. Often the reason is a past negative experience. Each customer also represents a significant amount of revenue over their lifetime. Learning to recognize what type of transaction each customer needs can help you to overcome customer's negative expectations. Recognizing that different people have different needs when it comes to the service transaction can help you and your employees meet, and exceed, customer expectations. More often than not, challenging customers can become your best, most loyal customers.

Handling Customer Types

Quadrant I Customers:

- Quick transactions.
- Don't need to know a lot about the service performed.
- Appear trusting.
- Having a vehicle serviced in an inconvenience.

You need to:

- ✓ Gather information quickly.
- ✓ Relay in a convenient manner what is wrong and what needs to be done.
- ✓ Make the transaction easy.
- ✓ Ensure Fixed Right First Time.

Quadrant II Customers:

- Prefer slower transactions
- Want to understand what was done and why
- May ask for old parts

You need to:

- ✓ Slow the process down.
- ✓ Explain in some detail what is wrong and what needs to be done.
- ✓ Make the transaction easy.
- ✓ Ensure Fixed Right First Time.

Handling Customer Types (cont'd)

Quadrant III Customers:

- Slowest of all transactions.
- May appear not to be trusting.
- Like to engage in conversation/storytelling.
- Can become excellent customers.

You need to:

- ✓ Slow the process down considerably.
- ✓ Explain in explicit detail what is wrong and what needs to be done.
- ✓ Show and tell with the customer.
- ✓ Ensure Fixed Right First Time

Quadrant IV Customers:

- People oriented, but prefer quick, efficient transactions.
- Ask pointed questions.
- Appear friendly, yet may be easily upset.
- Not likely to tell you why you've lost them as a customer.

You need to:

- ✓ Conduct an efficient transaction.
- ✓ Be thorough in gathering information and reviewing the invoice.
- ✓ Show and tell with the customer.
- ✓ Ensure Fixed Right First Time.

Meeting Customer Expectations

Understanding and learning to recognize that there are different types of customers is one thing, but with so many different types of customers and personalities in the world, how do we meet, and exceed, our customer's expectations?

Firstly, we can meet our customer's expectations by remembering what customer expectations are in general. When it comes to having a vehicle worked on, customers are specifically looking for:

- An accurate diagnosis
- An accurate and timely repair
- A fair price.

If you can meet these expectations alone, then you will have a leg up on many repair shops.

Secondly, add to the experience:

- Convenience
- Cleanliness
- The feeling of a personal touch

Adding these three additional attributes to the service experience will help you win a customer for life. That lifelong customer will bring you business time and again without having to expend exorbitant amounts of money on advertising and marketing.

As with everything in the universe, none of the previously listed expectations exists in isolation. Meeting a customer's expectations is a function of the entire business operation. Everyone from the technician, to the service writer, to the cashier, to the shuttle driver (if you have a shuttle service) is an important part of the solution. Like a championship sports team, if everyone does his or her job, the end result will be a satisfied customer.

> ### *Always Remember*
>
> - **Each customer is worth $200,000 or more to your repair shop.**
> - **Customers expect a bad experience. Surprise your customers by creating a positive service experience.**
> - **Customers come in different types with different needs. Pay attention to what each customer needs from the service experience and you will win a customer for life.**
> - **Customers want:**
>   - **An accurate diagnosis.**
>   - **An accurate and timely repair.**
>   - **A fair price**
>   - **Convenience**

Chapter 2: The Service Experience

In This Chapter

- **Scheduling appointments.**
- **The service write-up process.**
- **Estimating.**
- **Vehicle delivery process.**

After considering how the customer views the service experience, it's up to the repair shop to create an environment where customer expectations can be met and exceeded. Several factors and processes come into play when doing so. Technicians, service writers, and shop processes all play a crucial part in meeting expectations. The goal is always a happy, satisfied customer.

Scheduling

The aspect of automotive service repair that is most often overlooked is scheduling. Poor appointment scheduling is the root cause of many negative service experiences. It affects the transaction between the customer and service writer, affects the ability of the technician to make a proper diagnosis and repair, and will create an overall negative experience for the customer. Poor scheduling also keeps a shop from making the revenue and gross profit they are capable of.

Many bad experiences for both the customer, and the shop, can be avoided with proper scheduling practices. Scheduling, or shop loading, accomplishes a number of goals, all related to creating the best experience for every customer. The idea behind properly scheduling customers is not only to know how much work to expect on any given day, but to be able to allow time for service writers to communicate properly with each customer, and for the technicians to have the proper amount of time to execute a repair. Good scheduling will spread the workload throughout the day, and help to reduce intensely busy times or significant downtimes.

Something to Consider

An often overlooked key to customer satisfaction is a shop's scheduling practices. Carefully consider how you determine what vehicles to schedule and when to schedule them.

Good scheduling practices will also ensure a shop maximizes the number of vehicles worked on each day, without a roller coaster of light work, heavy work, carryover, etc. Great scheduling practices will help every employee recognize exactly how much work should be done each day, help customers feel taken care of, and allow a shop owner to plan proper budgets.

How does improper scheduling happen? How do you know what proper scheduling looks like? How many cars a day should a shop be working on?

Proper scheduling practices begin with a centralized schedule. It used to be, poor scheduling happened because multiple people were taking appointments and were not using a central appointment calendar. Today it is rare that a centralized, electronic, calendar isn't used, but know that anyone who may answer a phone to take an appointment should understand how to use the calendar. If for some reason you are not using an electronic calendar, or service management system software, always work from a single calendar.

Key Point

Everyone who can schedule customers must be subtracting from the same "time bucket" of available hours to properly load the shop each time an appointment is made.

The actual scheduling calendar may be a paper calendar that is shared, or an electronic calendar that is part of your shop management software. No matter what you use for a scheduling calendar, everyone who has access to it must understand how it is to be managed. This may take daily monitoring of the calendar to ensure that everyone with access to it is using it properly.

When I say "how the calendar is to be managed" I mean how many appointments can be made per time slot, how much time to allot for certain types of appointments, and when to avoid scheduling certain repair or diagnostic procedures. Every scheduling system must take into account not only those customers who will phone in an appointment, but those walk-in customers who will just "show up" each day. Trying to eliminate walk-in's, waiting customers, carryover, or tow in's is virtually impossible. It is far better to create a scheduling system that can easily manage these, than to try and control their possibility.

Determining how many appointments to schedule can sometimes be difficult. How many appointments your facility can handle per time slot will be dependent on how many service writers you employ, on the types of technicians you employ, and how productive those technicians are. Many computerized management systems will help you determine scheduling availability. If you do not use a computerized management system, you will need to determine for your shop, how many vehicles per time slot you want to schedule. This comes down to your experience and some guesswork, although I prefer to use actual math. Using math eliminates scheduling too lightly because you feel overwhelmed.

I strongly suggest purchasing a software-based shop management system. This will allow everyone who may be making appointments to work off the same calendar, as well as allow the shop to choreograph daily work in terms of who does the work, type of work brought in, and completion times. Some systems have the ability to program how much time to allot for each repair, or each technician, can calculate the optimum shop load, and ensure that the schedule is properly administered. These systems are not perfect and will require management creativity to ensure a process that is consistent and delivers the results you are looking for. If you have yet to purchase software, be sure to do your homework and prioritize those features most important to you. Spend some time with the scheduling portion of the software to find its strengths and weaknesses. Software-based shop management systems can take some of the guesswork out of proper scheduling, but never all of it.

If you are going to determine, for yourself, how many vehicles, and what type of repairs, to schedule per time slot, you will need to consider many factors:

- Average time per repair
- Average time per customer transaction
- Number of technicians
- Number of service writers
- Average number of carryover jobs

There are **two methods** you can use to determine how many customers to schedule each day. The Time Bucket Method is the most accurate, yet requires more daily management. The Repair Order Method is less time consuming, but may result in fewer billable hours produced.

Time Bucket Method of Scheduling

This method of scheduling not only allows you to be very accurate with exactly how many vehicles to book in a day, but takes it down to the detail of exactly what jobs to book. It's more time intensive, and requires some initial preparation, but can pay dividends when it comes to maximizing revenue and customer satisfaction.

To begin with, you must determine the actual amount of time it takes for your technicians to complete common repairs and maintenance services. Make a list of the most common repairs your shop executes. For the period of 1 month keep track, if you don't already, of how much time it takes your technicians to complete these common repairs and services. Include things such as:

- Oil changes
- Strut replacements
- Alignments
- Timing belts
- Tire rotations
- Tire changes
- Ball joint R&R
- Tie rod R&R
- Brake Inspections
- Front brake job
- Rear drum brake job
- Rear disc brake job
- EFI cleaning
- Maintenance services
- Other services commonly performed in your shop

Once you have the list of your most common services (the less common services you can use published times for), distribute the list to anyone who is allowed to schedule appointments. You'll use this list when scheduling to keep a running total of the hours you've scheduled for any given day. If you only use published times, you may well end up with less than a maximum number of hours that could have been produced on any given day.

You must track the actual amount of time that these jobs take. Be sure not to shortcut the process. Explain to your employees why you are doing this, and have your technicians take accurate time punches. Don't just ask your technicians how long these jobs take, or use anecdotal times. These may or may not be accurate. You want to know the average amount of time each job really takes. Collecting good data will allow you to make good decisions, and put good processes in place.

Most computerized management systems will allow you to allocate a certain amount of time per job code. Be sure your system reflects the proper times. If you're using a paper schedule, develop, and post a list of these commonly scheduled operations with their associated times so that each person who is scheduling an appointment has easy access to them.

Now that you know how much time (approximately) each common job will take, it's time to understand how many hours each day, or week, you'll want to schedule. You can do this a couple of different ways.

The first is to use a "theoretical" time number to get to your Theoretical Shop Capacity. This assumes each technician will produce a certain amount of billable time in a day.

The second is to know exactly what the average number of billable hours your shop can produce is. In the industry this number is known as Shop Capacity or Productive Capacity.

Here are the formulas:

Theoretical Shop Capacity

#Techs x 8hours x Days Open = Billable Hours/Week

Actual Shop Capacity

#Techs x 8hours x Days Open x Avg. Shop Production % =
Billable Hours/Week

To calculate the Actual Shop Capacity, you'll have to know
your shop's Average Shop Production %. This can be calculated using:

Hours Billed / Hours Worked x 100

You can use any time period you want for these numbers. Of
course the longer the time period, the more accurate the number. For instance, during a single day, a shop of four technicians works a total of thirty two hours over the course of the
day (four technicians x eight hours each). These four technicians produce forty-three billable hours.

43 Hours Billed / 32 Hours Worked x 100 = 134%

To use this and calculate the Actual Shop Capacity we would
apply the formula on the previous page.

4 Techs x 8 Hours x 5 Days Open x 134% = 214.4 Hours

This means that, based on our one-day Shop Production percentage, we could produce 214 hours of work in any given week. Of course, this may, or may not, be reasonable. We would want to look at this over a longer period of time. Let's say we look at a month's worth of data.

During August of the previous year we see that our same four technicians produced 702 billable hours, while working 678 hours. This means we had a 103% production percentage. (702 Hours Billed ÷ 678 Hours Worked x 100). If we apply the 103% to our previous formula we find that we can, assuming the same technicians and similar conditions, expect to produce 165 hours over a week's time period.

If we can expect to produce (or bill) 165 hours per week, then we know we should schedule this many hours. Knowing how long each job takes, every time a customer calls to schedule an appointment, we look up how long that job takes, and subtract it from our "time bucket" of 165 hours.

A challenge with this method of scheduling is that it requires math! It also requires manual tracking of the "time bucket" in most shops. Furthermore, the first pushback anyone gives is "yeah, but what about carryover work, tow in's, walk-in's, upsells, etc.?" You can work around these issues by subtracting from the time bucket (in our example: 165 hours) a number for upsells, tow in's, etc. Maybe you only schedule 120 hours on the schedule to allow for these other conditions.

At the beginning of every day, you, or your software system, must subtract from this total "time bucket" any carryover jobs from the day before, and any already scheduled appointments, to obtain today's working available time. This is now the available amount of time you have for new appointments to be scheduled for today. Appointments being scheduled into the future, of course, cannot account for any carryover jobs.

In either case, although this method creates excellent habits of knowing exactly what your shop production is, exactly how many hours your technicians can handle, and an awareness of the overall efficiency of your organization, it is overwhelming for many shops to adopt.

> **Key Point**
>
> Be sure to quantify exactly how much time the common jobs your shop performs take. Doing so anecdotally can compound scheduling challenges.

One method some shops use to get around the overwhelm, is to only assign a certain amount of time to each person scheduling. Now that you know how many hours of time you have available to be scheduled each day, you can choose how you want the time allocated. Small shops, with a small number of individuals doing the scheduling, may choose to work from one schedule. This requires each scheduler to subtract the appropriate amount of time from the total time available so that everyone understands how much time is left for any particular day. You can imagine what challenges might occur should someone not be keeping track of how much time is left!

Larger shops may choose to divide the total available time among each service writer and let them fill their own "bucket" each day. This can create some confusion, and the occasional trading of time. It also assumes that each "team" of technician and service writer is somewhat equal in what they can produce. Technician and service writer pay plans may also enter into the decision to treat scheduling in this manner.

A good scheduling system is a dynamic one. It constantly needs to be adjusted based on the work currently in the shop, upsell opportunities, and employees who may be unexpectedly out for the day. When you are scheduling service appointments you can't necessarily account for what will happen in the future, but by having an understanding of what your schedule capacity is, you can help to smooth out your workflow which will result in increased customer satisfaction and will maximize your shop productivity and revenue.

Repair Order Method of Scheduling

A simpler, and some would say, much more useable method of scheduling is what I call the Repair Order Method. This is the method I use with most of the shops I coach. This method is not as accurate, and relies more heavily on averages, but is much easier to manage and maintain.

Begin by knowing how many hours per time period you do, or want to, produce. For example, if over the course of one month, your shop produced 630 hours of billable time you can reasonably expect this to be done again. However, how does this relate to how many customers to schedule?

The next bit of data you need to know is what your average Hours Per Repair Order are. If we have an average of 2.3 hours for each repair order (over the same time period, or any time period), we then divide the hours produced, by the hours per repair order to get a number of repair orders, or number of customers. In our example we would take $630 \div 2.3 = 274$ customers. We now divide this number by the number of days in the month we were using to obtain the 630 hours. In this case let's say it was 21 days. 274 customers $\div 21 = 13$ customers per day.

Does this make rational sense? If we have four technicians, working on 13 cars each day means each one will have to work on roughly 3 cars apiece. In my experience this seems to make sense, but....what about oil changes?

In theory, using our 630 hour number already accounted for oil changes, as did our 2.3 hours/repair order number (because to get to these numbers, there must have been oil changes done during these repairs, or in other words, at least some of those 630 hours were just oil change repair orders).

Because the math can be hard to see and sometimes it doesn't feel intuitive, I will generally suggest that a shop schedule 1/3 of total number of vehicles as oil changes. With an ability to work on 13 cars a day, in this case we would schedule 10 cars and 3 oil changes.

One last adjustment that can be made here is to lower the total number of appointments to account for walk-in's or tow-in's if you want to. If a shop has a couple of people a day who just show up, then schedule 8 vehicles and 3 oil changes – and hope two more cars show up. Try to quantify how many walk-ins or tow-ins the shop has during a month. I always tell my coaching clients, I never want to hear "I feel like" or "I think". Too often we are wrong until we look at the numbers.

The danger in not sticking with what the math tells you can be done is that you'll lose money if you schedule too lightly, too often. At the end of the month, or year, this can hurt. Remember, automotive service shops sell time. Once the physical time has gone by, and no work was done, you can never bill for that time again.

Proper scheduling is nothing more than another name for time management. You are trying to manage the hours of the day so that your technicians stay busy, but are not too busy that customer satisfaction suffers. Furthermore, you are trying to manage the hours of the day so that your service writers have the appropriate amount of time to spend with your customers. Finally, you are trying to manage the hours of the day so that your customers don't need to wait an exorbitant amount of time for their vehicle to be repaired. All of this means being as intentional as you can with your schedule. This is done by knowing how many hours a month, or week, the shop should be producing.

Schedule Efficiency

There is a metric that can be used to monitor how well you are using your schedule in terms of shop production. This metric is called Schedule Efficiency. Like many efficiency metrics it is nothing more than a mathematical comparison of what could be done and what is being done. To calculate Schedule Efficiency, divide the number of repair orders completed in a week by the number of customers that needed to be scheduled. Multiply this result by 100 to get a percentage.

For example:

Our four technicians billed a total of 145 hours last week, over 72 repair orders. Based on a historical number of 80 repairs orders this week, and our current 2.1 hours/repair orders, we expected to produce (schedule) 168 hours, or 80 repair orders. In looking at last week's schedule, we see that instead of booking 16 customers each day (80 repair orders divided by 5 days), we only booked an average of 12 customers each day.

Therefore, our Schedule Efficiency is: (72 ÷ 80) x 100 = 90%

Ninety percent does not seem too far off. Let's think about what this means. If we wanted 80 repair orders but only completed 72, we were 8 customers off for the week. If our Average Repair Order dollars (explained in a later chapter), is $515 per repair order, we left $4,120 on the table this week. Over the course of a year, this means $206,000.

You can see that even a 10% margin in Schedule Efficiency can result in big dollars at the end of a business year. Always strive for a 100% Schedule Efficiency number. If you are consistently in the +100% range, it likely means you are underestimating how many vehicles you can work on in a week.

As a consultant friend of mine was fond of saying "plan for the ordinary, and manage the extraordinary". In other words, don't worry about accounting for the unseen. Plan the schedule based on real numbers, and make adjustments when jobs take longer than expected, someone calls in sick, or a big upsell occurs. This can take some mental discipline, but I promise that it will help to maximize your shop's productivity, profit, and customer satisfaction.

Proper scheduling can make everyone involved in the repair process more relaxed, more efficient, and will generate higher levels of customer satisfaction. Higher levels of customer satisfaction will make you more money!

The Service Write-up Process

Proper scheduling gets the service process off to a great start. The service write-up process is the next link in ensuring a positive customer service experience. This may be the most critical link in satisfying customers, and is often the link in the service chain where things go wrong.

Customer Satisfaction Point

The service write up process is the most important aspect of your business affecting customer satisfaction. If you pay no attention to anything else, do what you must to ensure a good write up experience for the customer.

The service write-up process is the key point of contact between the repair shop and customer. The tone of the entire service experience is set during the write up process. If you decide not to pay attention to any other aspect of the service experience, (which I'm not suggesting you do), then focus all of your attention on your service write-up process.

The service write-up process includes:

1. Greeting the customer

2. Gathering information for diagnosis

3. Gathering information for the sale process (as well as customer relationship building)

4. Confirming customer data (phone, email, address)

5. Educating the Customer

6. Selling needed Service, Maintenance, and Repairs.

7. Communication

8. Invoicing the Customer

The individual(s) who handle this transaction are critical to setting customer expectations, gathering information for the technician to be able to do his or her job, successfully selling to the customer, and in ensuring that the customer has a great experience. I cannot emphasize enough the importance of the service write-up process and the people who make that happen.

The service write-up process should be consistent, timely,
and set the tone for the customer's service experience. The
customer wants to leave the process feeling that they were listened to, that their concerns will be resolved, and confident
that their vehicle will be well taken care of. The image the
customer carries away from this process will be the image
they hold of your repair facility.

So how can the service writer help to create a positive customer experience that is consistent, pleasant, and provides a
sense of satisfaction for all types of customers? Let's take the
process step by step.

The Greeting

Ask that your service writers focus on one customer at a time
and greet each customer pleasantly and appropriately. It
doesn't matter what greeting they use as long as it is pleasant.
Sometimes it is challenging to greet customers pleasantly
when things get busy, but doing so can change the entire
transaction. If there is a line of customers at the counter, making quick eye contact with the next person in line and saying,
"I'll be right with you ma'am" can set the tone for everyone
in line. It says, "I'm aware that all of you are here, and will
get to you as soon as I'm finished with this equally important

customer". The last thing you want to do is ignore a customer at the counter.

Customers are always listening even when they are not the one being addressed. If a customer hears an exasperated service writer dealing with another customer, then they expect to be treated in the same manner and a negative expectation is set. If they hear a cordial service writer, the expectation becomes something entirely different.

As difficult as it may be at times, your service writers should do their best to put on a smile, maintain some semblance of order, and appear positive. The attitude and demeanor of your service writer will significantly contribute to the customer's overall service experience, as well as their willingness to purchase suggested services. If the customer walks away feeling like the service writer was busy, hassled, and not happy to be there, then the customer will be unsure of whether they were listened to and will likely be expecting the worst.

If the customer walks away feeling like the service writer was happy, in control, and really cared about their concerns, then this will set a completely different tone. It will instill confidence in the customer that their concerns will be addressed and that their vehicle is in good hands. Never underestimate the importance of attitude and facial expressions during the greeting!

Something to Consider

Active listening can be a key to making a customer feel heard. Eye contact, head nodding, smiles, and the expression of empathy can go a long way in creating a positive customer experience.

You could have a noisy, dingy, messy waiting area and if the customer greeting goes well, the customer won't even notice! *That is how important the greeting process is. It truly sets the tone of the entire service experience.*

Never forget, people do business with people, not with businesses. This is easy to overlook when you're ridiculously busy and customers just seem to keep coming through the door, or the phone keeps ringing. You prefer to deal with

---

Key Point

Always take the time to explain the repair to the customer. You don't want a customer walking out the door not knowing why they just paid the amount of money they did!

---

pleasant customer service people in your own life, so you must try to separate yourself from the feelings in the moment and provide the customer with a great, feel-good, experience.

Telephone Greeting

When answering the phone, it's even more important to set a tone with the customer. It's estimated that over 80 percent of your customers will call before visiting for the first time. This means that the first contact most customers will have with your shop is over the telephone. I like to think of the telephone greeting as part of your branding as well.

Phones can get busy at the shop, which means everyone needs to be prepared to answer the phone. We live in a time when customers don't want to leave a voicemail, expect someone to answer the phone when they call, and pay attention to how the phone is answered. Standardizing your greeting is important. I suggest everyone who answers the phone (technicians as well) greet the customer pleasantly, express the name of the shop, tell the caller who they're talking to and express and interest in helping. Here's an example:

"Good Morning, XYZ Automotive, Greg speaking, how may I help you?"

This is simple, easy, and anyone can learn to use these words. When the phones start ringing on a Monday morning every time they get answered, customers should here the same thing!

Active Listening

Whether it's on the phone, or in person, a great customer experience continues with listening. Listening also ensures you collect solid data regarding what the customer is concerned about, what may be important to them (thus getting you a sale), and any changes in their contact information that must be noted in your shop management system.

When I say listening, I mean not just listening, but *actively listening* to the customer. Look the customer in the eye, appear interested, and repeat back to them what you heard them say. Fully engage your customer when listening to their concerns.

There are three steps to Active Listening:

1. Make eye contact.

2. Nod your head.

3. Mirroring.

Making eye contact helps the customer to understand that you are really listening to them. We all like to think we are good at multitasking, and even if you are, doing something else other than looking a customer in the eye while listening will lead them to believe you are not listening. (At this point in time, data shows that humans aren't actually all that good at multi-tasking, so focusing on one thing at a time helps you as much as the customer experience).

You've experienced someone who wouldn't look you in the eye when they talked to you. How did it make you feel? No doubt it was awkward at best. The computer terminals that we use today to collect information and make our lives easier have also had a negative effect on the customer feeling listened to. Often, I recommend using a notepad to take notes instead of the keyboard because it is easier to maintain eye contact with a customer when doing so. When a customer sees you taking notes, they understand you are listening. I've known shop managers who didn't like the use of notebooks because when they'd had to cover for someone who was out, they couldn't decipher what the service writer had written. To me this isn't a good reason not to use one – you'll be using it more yourself than anyone else will. The point of writing things down in front of a customer was once driven home to me during an interview I conducted.

I once tried to engage in an interview with an executive by taking notes on my smartphone. At the end of the interview, the person looked at me and said "Can I give you one bit of advice? Take notes in a notepad. It will give the person you're interviewing a much better feeling than using your phone." She was right. I believe this holds true at the service counter as well. Note taking, while making eye contact, contact makes a huge difference in how the customer feels, and the level of engagement by the service advisor. This alone will result in better information being gathered.

The second step to Active Listening, nodding your head as you are listening, seems silly, yet there is some very real psychology behind it. Humans interpret head nodding as "yes, this is true". By you nodding your head during the conversation with a customer not only do you send the message that you are listening, but the customer feels empowered that they are doing the right thing. It also helps send the message that the both of you are in agreement.

Of course, if we are talking about Active Listening while on the telephone, head nodding doesn't have the same effect. The effect it does have, however, is on the service advisor. Just like smiling while you talk on the phone creates a different tone, so does head nodding while on the phone. Head nodding creates a higher engagement level with the conversation.

The third step, mirroring, is just as useful when listening in person as it is over the telephone. Mirroing helps both you and the customer. It is as important in making the customer feel heard as it is in collecting information, and it will help you collect better, and more, information. Mirroring is saying back to the customer the last one, two, or three words you heard them say to you – and then pausing. Nobody likes that pause, and we all will try to fill the silence. What you'll hear a customer do, is fill in what they perceive as a gap in information.

Here's an example conversation:

SA: "Mrs. Smith, tell me how you use your vehicle on a regular basis."

Mrs. Smith: "Just around town and to deliver groceries on Wednesday."

SA (using mirroring): "Deliver groceries?"

Mrs. Smith: "Yes, my church helps elderly people who can't get out of their house much to do their grocery shopping every Wednesday."

By using mirroring, you've not only gathered information regarding how Mrs. Smith uses her vehicle, but what might be important to her. Sometimes the information comes in the form of exactly when a problem occurs, how often a problems occurs, or some other bit of info that the technician can use to get to a root cause of a problem.

Mirroing also allows a customer to hear, in their words, what was just said. Often a customer may realize that what you thought they said, (or what they thought they said), wasn't what was meant and will provide more information to clarify things.

Key Point

Mirroring is saying back to a customer the last couple of words they just said to you, with a question mark, and then waiting for them to answer.

Mirroring is a great way to gather more information regarding what a customer is concerned about, or what is important to them.

Do not underestimate how important listening to the customer during the initial write-up process is. Just like smiling and appearing positive, actively listening to your customer will leave them with a sense of confidence that their concerns will be addressed. This will pay dividends for you later, when, during the repair process, you need to sell the repair or explain the cost of the repair.

Key Point

There are three steps to Active Listening:

1. Make eye contact.

2. Nod your head.

3. Mirroring.

When it comes time to sell the repair you'll not only need to listen to the customer concern but you will need to impart some knowledge regarding the suggested repairs or services to your customer. If the customer feels like you've previously listened to them, they will be more open to listening to you at this point and it will make your sales job easier.

The bottom line is that good communication between the service writer and the customer begins with active listening. Really listening to each and every customer will help the repair process go smoothly and will ensure that the customer starts off the service visit with a good experience.

Check out the video Active Listening on my YouTube channel for tips and techniques to improving your Active

Listening Skills. It's one of the most important skills you can develop!

Information Collection

During the service write-up process your service writer(s) must obtain three sets of important information: customer information, vehicle information, and problem information. All three of these information sets are crucial to a positive customer experience and Active Listening is key to gathering solid information. Information such as customer contact and vehicle identification can be fairly straightforward while information regarding customer concern and problem analysis can be more challenging. Be sure to give your service writer the tools they need to make this part of the write-up process consistent and thorough.

Customer Information

Ask that your service writers confirm critical customer information such as the telephone number where they can be reached, a physical mailing address, and an email address.

Customer Satisfaction Point

Make sure your customer knows that you are collecting their contact information so that they may be quickly reached to expedite their repair.

Have the service writer explain to the customer that they are collecting this information so that the customer can be quickly reached if more information is needed, or when the repair estimate is ready for their approval.

If you have written policies outlining how the customer's contact information will be protected it's a good idea to let the customer know this as well. Always allow a customer to opt out of being contacted in a certain manner, or with certain material. This shows the customer that you are collecting this information in good faith and will only use it in a manner that they find acceptable. Never violate the customer's confidence in the name of potential profits or marketing!

The service writer should always ask how the customer prefers to be reached so that important information can be relayed in order to ensure a timely repair to the vehicle. It doesn't do the shop, or the customer, any good to finally be able to reach the customer at four in the afternoon when parts can't be acquired until the next day, or the technician no longer has time left in the day to perform the repair. Understanding how best to contact the customer is crucial to maintaining a positive customer experience.

Key Point

Always obtain a customer's email and their preferred method of contact!

Many customers today are as easily (and sometimes more conveniently) contacted via email as they are via telephone. Collecting email addresses can also help you with building your marketing database for future marketing efforts. By confirming the telephone number and email address each time the customer comes in valuable time can be saved when trying to contact the customer later on with a repair estimate or the okay to do the job. Verifying this information will also ensure your database is always up to date.

Collecting and confirming this information should become second nature to your service desk employees.

Vehicle Information

Collecting vehicle information is important for a number of reasons. It's important to the technician so that he or she can save repair time. It is important to the service writer so that they can organize and record each vehicle being checked in. It is important to the repair shop so that customer demographics and targeted marketing practices can be developed.

```
┌─────────────────────────────────────────┐
│              Key Point                    │
│                                           │
│  Collecting accurate customer concern     │
│  information is crucial to avoiding       │
│  multiple repair attempts!                │
│                                           │
└─────────────────────────────────────────┘
```

From the technician's perspective, having the VIN, mileage, and license plate numbers on the repair order can save valuable technician time during the repair process. Technicians will use this information while they are looking up service information or researching parts price and availability. Many parts suppliers today need VIN information to properly identify which part is needed for a repair. It can also save technicians time when locating a vehicle in a crowded parking lot, or if the vehicle is parked on the street amongst many other vehicles.

From a service writer's perspective, collecting vehicle information will help to avoid confusion should customers have similar names, or have more than one vehicle being serviced at the shop. You'd be amazed at how many customer names are similar, or how many white Chevrolet Malibu's there are in existence!

Key Point

Collecting and storing vehicle information can be extremely useful in making management decisions.

Collecting vehicle information is also important for repair shop management purposes. Repair shops that utilize a computerized management system, (if you are not one of them, you should be considering becoming one), are often able to mine the system for vehicle and customer data to better target marketing efforts. Having this data available may also help you with stocking inventory with commonly used parts, and making decisions as to what type of shop equipment to purchase.

Customer Satisfaction Point

Information regarding the customer's concern is extremely important. Use active listening techniques and a Customer Problem Analysis Sheet to collect important information.

Customer Concern Information

The next batch of information the service writer(s) must collect relates to the service the customer has brought the vehicle to your shop to have performed. This is where active listening is critical to creating an overall positive customer experience! Too many service writers remain hidden behind their computer terminals at this point. Service desk employees should get away from their computer terminals and engage in active listening while the customer is relaying this crucial information!

If there is one area that customers will be completely tuned into its whether or not the repair shop fixed their car right the first time they brought it in. We've already gone through the list of reasons that customers hate bringing their car in for service or repair and at the top of the list is inconvenience. If they feel inconvenienced the first time they bring the vehicle to your shop for a repair, imagine how they are going to feel when they have to bring it back for a second time! *Collecting customer concern information is crucial to avoiding multiple repair attempts.*

Taking the time to collect and document customer concern information at the time of write-up can eliminate costly problems, and customer satisfaction problems, later. It is up to everyone who contacts the customer, and works on the vehicle to help ensure a "fixed right first time" experience.

Fixed Right First Time

"Fixed right first time" is a key component to customer satisfaction. The problem could be something as simple as the Maintenance Reminder Light is still on after the oil change. This might be no big deal to you or your technicians, but to a customer this represents a significant error. Generally they see a light on and know something isn't right. Any reason at all for unexpectedly returning to the repair shop represents a negative experience.

There are many ways to ensure a "fixed right first time" customer experience. A tool I suggest providing your service writer(s) with is a Customer Problem Analysis Sheet (see Appendix C). Utilizing a Customer Problem Analysis Sheet to gather information from a customer serves two purposes.

> ### Key Point
>
> Stress to your technicians that they must be thorough even when making "routine" repairs. Warning lights on after a repair are always a concern for a customer.

First, it gathers critical information for the technician who will be performing the service on the vehicle. Many times a service writer may not know exactly what information will be useful to the technician. Utilizing a Customer Problem Analysis Sheet will encourage the service writer to collect all of the information every time a vehicle is presented with a concern. This avoids spending time later in the day trying to reach the customer and gather information not previously acquired.

> ### Customer Satisfaction Point
>
> Utilizing a Customer Problem Analysis Sheet can help gather pertinent information as well as make the customer feel like they had some input in the repair process.
>
> See Appendix C.

Secondly, it helps the customer feel heard. The customer gets to see someone writing down what they say the problem is, and gets to provide information important and relevant to the diagnostic or service process. With a service writer typing away on a computer where the screen can't be seen, the customer doesn't really know what information is being relayed.

By filling out a Customer Problem Analysis Sheet with the customer, or asking the customer to take a minute and answer the questions on the sheet by themselves, not only can valuable information be gathered, but it can help the customer feel empowered and a part of the diagnostic process. The same Customer Problem Analysis Sheet can be used when attending to MIL 'on' repairs. Many repair shop information systems such as Alldata, or Mitchell, have extensive information sheets for drivability problems, or MIL 'on' concerns, which can be used. Use these sheets to collect information, but be aware that trying to collect too much information can sometimes be more of a burden than a help.

Key Point

Never assume the current customer's problem is the same as the problem presented by another customer last week.

Have your technician suggest what information from these sheets is most useful to them, and only collect that information. Customers will be less likely to supply very much helpful information other than if the light ever goes out, or whether it ever blinks. There are times when they may be able to associate an event that seemed related to the MIL coming on, but this is rare and depends entirely on the customer's awareness. Don't underestimate the importance of including the customer in the repair of the vehicle at this point. You'd be amazed at how far this can go towards making a customer feel more at ease when having their vehicle serviced.

"Fixed right first time" starts with information gathering. This is especially critical when it comes to intermittent problems. Your technicians are taught that the first step in the diagnostic process is to Verify the Concern (see Appendix G). In order for the technician to legitimately verify the concern they need to understand when, where, and how the customer is experiencing the problem. Sometimes the customer's concern is very apparent, while at other times it can be questionable as to exactly what the customer is concerned with.

Encourage your service writers to never assume they know what the customer is complaining about. Just because a problem sounds like something that came in last week, doesn't mean it's anywhere near the same problem. There are many times that the customer will need to show the service writer, or the technician, exactly what the problem is. This can be challenging because of time constraints within the shop, personnel resources, or the physical location of the repair shop lending itself to a quick and easy test drive.

Do what you can to create time for your service writer to fully understand the customer's concern. This may mean giving the service writer the time they need to walk out to the vehicle with the customer. Put a process in place that will allow your writer to do this while someone else covers the desk. As inconvenient as it may sound to do something like this, it can save valuable time later in the day. It's also one of those "personal touches" that can go a long way in creating happy customers.

If the shop really and truly doesn't have the immediate personnel or time resources at hand to allow for a test drive with
the customer, the service writer should take the time to ask as
many questions of the vehicle driver (utilizing the Customer
Problem Analysis Sheet) as they can. Try and give the technician as much information as possible regarding how to get the
vehicle to exhibit the problem symptoms.

Notice that I say, "vehicle driver". This is because often times
the individual that brings the vehicle into the repair shop is
not the actual driver of the vehicle. The vehicle may be
driven daily by the wife or husband of a family, but for many
different reasons it is the occasional driver of the vehicle who
brings it in for service. This is an important distinction since
the person the service writer is acquiring information from
may not have all of the information. If you suspect that this is
the case, then ask permission to contact the driver of the vehicle and fill out the Customer Problem Analysis Sheet over the
phone.

Another critical part of "fixed right first time" is the communication between the service writer and the technician. There
are many pitfalls that occur here. A service writer must be
able to translate what the customer is saying into language
that the technician can understand, as well as interpret what
the technician is asking the service writer or customer. This is

never an easy job. The Customer Problem Analysis Sheet can help with this.

Something to Consider

When collecting customer concern information, don't assume the person at the counter is the regular driver of the vehicle.

Something that every service writer needs to learn to avoid is to "diagnose on the drive". This means that the service writer needs to be conscious of only collecting the information that the customer is giving them and not to draw any conclusions from it. Let the technician do his or her job. Just because the symptoms sound the same as the vehicle that came in last week that needed a wheel bearing, doesn't mean that's the problem with this vehicle. Provide the customer complaint information to the technician and let the technician make a diagnosis.

Something to Consider

Encourage your service writers to ask the technician to show them the problem and demonstrate the solution.

On the other side of that challenge is interpreting what the technician is asking the service writer to find out from the customer. Many questions that a technician might ask are rather standard and can be listed on a Customer Problem

Analysis Sheet, however every situation is different. A technician might have a very specific question regarding the vehicle in question. If a service writer is in doubt about exactly what the technician is asking, I suggest having the technician write it down word-for-word and the service writer just read it as it's written to the customer.

Taking time with the customer, actively listening to the customer, and not making assumptions are all part of collecting the appropriate information regarding the customer concern. Understanding exactly what the customer is complaining about can be difficult, but is critical to "fixed right the first time."

Selling and Educating

The next step in the service write-up process revolves around selling service, maintenance, and repairs to a customer. Your greeting and listening skills established a strong foundation for your customer relationship. What comes next will vary from customer to customer, but it will not be successful without this strong base.

Auto repair shops exist because customer are willing to spend money to ensure their vehicle stays on the road, keeps it's resale value, gets them where they are going, or is safe in many different driving conditions. This willingness to spend money comes from how much they trust you, how much they learn about what is wrong and what needs to be done, and how well you can explain the processes required during the service process.

Although there is a process to selling, and a large amount of psychology when it comes to successful selling, much selling is nothing more than educating a customer.

The Importance of Education

During most of the service write up process you will be educating the customer. Whether you are selling, showing the Courtesy Inspection, or answering questions you are educating. Often, education takes place passively while the customer sits in the waiting area and watches AutoNet TV, reads the material you've left there, or overhears the conversations at the service counter. You are always educating. This is really important in not only getting the sale, but in reducing a customer's anxiety.

We all have an inherent fear, or anxiety, of the unknown. Not knowing, or not understanding can create a number of emotional reactions from a customer. Everything from a customer pretending to understand, to an angry, accusatory reaction from a customer, can come from a fear of the unknown. Nobody likes to think that they don't know something and very few of us will ever admit when we don't know something. Often our fear shows itself as aggression, arrogance, or annoyance. It's been said that the hardest three words for a human to speak are "I don't know". Because this can be so hard, and customers don't want to be taken advantage of because they don't know something, they will often not say anything at all.

Along with a pleasant attitude and listening to a customer, imparting some knowledge of the situation can go a long way in building trust and a great relationship that benefits you and the customer. Just telling the customer what they "need" or what you did to fix the problem, often isn't enough to make a customer feel empowered. Many customers need a better understanding of what the problem is, what caused the problem, and how the repair will resolve their concern. Never assume a customer understands what you are describing, or telling them.

I can't tell you how many phone calls I get from upset friends who just spent a large amount of money to have their car worked on. When I ask what the shop did, they answer with "how do I know"? If the repair had been properly explained to them, they most likely wouldn't be as upset about spending the money!

Something to Consider

Use one of the many virtual products available today to demonstrate to the customer what is wrong and what needs to be done!

Assuming that most customers have a poor understanding at best, of all things mechanical, it's often helpful to have some sort of visual aide to help in the explanation. There are many different visual aids available to help the service writer explain certain vehicle systems and repairs. Whether it is a laminated poster, flip chart, or animated computer software, each can help the customer visualize what the service writer is describing.

I'll make a note about Google and YouTube here. Customers are going to use these tools to get their own information. Our industry laughs and jokes about it, or gets very annoyed and upset when customers use these sources to empower themselves. Customers will use them. Get over it. You and I use them too! If you are concerned about where a customer got his or her information, then use these tools together. Show your customer where they can get credible information, have the information available on your own website, or use third-party software that demonstrates the concepts, systems, and necessary repairs. Customers only take to internet resources to help them feel empowered and less likely to be taken advantage of. Embrace their need for more education and come prepared with electronic resources of your own.

A very helpful practice, often considered "old school" now, is having a roll cart of new and used parts to show a customer. Common repair items such as shocks, struts, brake pads, air filters, spark plugs, etc. can be displayed in the waiting area to help educate a customer. Some shops have created wall decorations using new and used parts wire-tied to pegboard to both give their customers something to look at while they are waiting and the service writer something to utilize during a repair explanation.

If you choose to create a wall of parts, or just have a roll cart accessible to the customer, make sure you've done your best to label the parts. Also be sure that there are no hazardous edges on any of the components on display. Clean the parts up, protect anything sharp or hazardous from the customer, and display them professionally. You'll be amazed at how much of a help old parts can be in selling new parts! It also helps in keeping customers out of the service bays, and is far more effective, and less of an affront, than the "no customers allowed in the service area" signs you see in many repair shops. Just because you'd rather use the virtual tools available today, doesn't mean seeing, or touching, an actual part won't appeal to your customer!

When it comes to educating the different customer types, try to be sure that during the service writer's explanation of the problem, and resolution, that the customer doesn't feel they are being talked down to. This can be a little bit of a gray area. Some customers don't want to admit what they don't know, while other customers may tell you that they know something they really don't know. The service writer will have to determine for themselves how much the customer wants to know, needs to know, and how to deliver that knowledge. The more practice a service writer has, the easier it will get to read the customer. A good service writer can read the customer and deliver knowledge without the customer ever feeling talked down to or confused by too technical an explanation.

Key Point

Customers rarely admit when they don't know something. It is better to explain too much, than risk the customer walking away not knowing what they need to.

Listening to a customer and providing basic knowledge so that the customer feels empowered to make a decision can take time. In a busy shop, service writers may not always feel like they have the time, but these two actions are critical to high levels of customer satisfaction. Eventually the time spent listening to the customer, and providing knowledge to the customer, will pay off as you'll create a customer who is no longer apprehensive about coming to the shop. Customers who return again and again to spend money with you are what you want. It is far better to slow the write-up process and create these customers, than it is to constantly feel hassled and have to constantly conquest new customers.

The Customer Buying Process

To understand the true importance of educating the customer, as well as listening actively to your customers, you must understand the Customer Buying Process. Actively listening, educating, and knowing the process each of us goes through in our head when we buy something leads to successful sales. All businesses are built on successful sales.

The Customer Buying Process is well researched psychology that every customer, including you and I, goes through when we purchase something. If any of the steps are incomplete for us, we are unlikely to purchase something, or if we do make a purchase, we are likely to be unhappy with that purchase. You are welcome to find all the research, white papers, and textbooks written on why customers purchased certain products. In the case that you don't wish to do that, I've boiled the process down to these five steps:

1. **Need Recognition**

2. **Gather Information**

3. **Determine Alternatives and Options**

4. **Decision Making**

5. **Post-purchase behavior**

This process is followed, in order, by the brain when deciding whether to make a purchase or not. You, as service writer, must learn to support each of these steps, and most importantly, recognize where in this process a customer is in order to successfully sell. Let's take a look at each of these steps in more detail.

Need Recognition

For each of us, this step is where we realize that we need something. You could argue that this might be a "want", yet what do we tend to do with "wants"? We often make wants into "needs".

The "gee, it'd be nice to have a new truck" often becomes a running list in our heads of what's wrong with our current truck. This list grows, and becomes more immediate, the longer we think about having a new truck. Eventually we get the point of saying things like "this truck isn't worth putting more money into" or "it's just not getting the job done anymore".

In either case, our brain, and your customer's brain must recognize that something new is needed. Remember, however, that just telling someone that they "need" something is not creating Need Recognition. We each must come to the recognition that we need something on our own.

Sometimes we recognize the need for service, maintenance, or repair of our automobile because it dies on the road, a light comes on (and flashes at us), or a funny noise or vibration shows up. Other times, we only recognize the need for something when someone points out to us that we need something done. If that person is a trusted individual in our lives, we'll immediately establish Need Recognition. If that person has yet to become a highly trusted individual, we may need more education about what's wrong, why, and what needs to be done.

In terms of selling to automotive service customers, keep in mind that often you need to sell something the customer has no idea that they need. Therefore, your job is to help the customer create Need Recognition. This is where your ability to educate a customer becomes very important.

You will use tools such as pictures, videos, animated software, actual parts, etc. to educate the customer about what is wrong with their current situation, and what executing a needed repair will do to improve the situation. You will often use "show and tell" with the customer. Walking the customer to their vehicle, showing them the problem, while giving a verbal explanation, will often be enough to get a customer to agree to a sale. With enough education regarding what went wrong, why it went wrong, and what needs to be done, the customer will realize that something really does need to be done, and thus have Need Recognition.

The words you use to communicate with your customer can be important in establishing Need Recognition as well. We'll discuss a complete selling scenario later, but for now, know that saying things like "you may have noticed" can help the customer connect something they've noticed about the operation of their automobile with something you are suggesting be serviced, or repaired.

Gather Information

The next step in the Customer Buying Process is where the customer figures out who can help. Maybe they've taken the first step of Need Recognition because Uncle Joe suggested they need an alignment due to obvious tire wear. The question they may have no is "who does alignments".

Often, Gathering Information is confused with getting the details of a repair, or calling a shop and saying "how much does X service cost". Although these are ways to gather information, this specific step in the Customer Buying Process is all about "who can help with this Need".

The auto repair shop will influence this step of the Customer Buying Process through their marketing, signage, word-of-mouth, and website. This second step in the process every customer goes through, is why marketing your repair shop is so incredibly important. Many shops don't conduct effective marketing and may miss customers who have recognized a need, but failed to recognize your shop can help!

The service writer can influence this step of the process by making sure customers know how to use your shop's Customer Referral Program, utilizing your website to educate customers on the types of services you offer, and providing exceptional levels of customer satisfaction (to drive those word-of-mouth referrals).

Remember, when customers recognize a need for something they will often turn to friends, family, and co-workers to find out who can help. These people tend to be trusted members of our network. When we need a new roof, new windows, or a new computer, we often reach out to those we know, and trust, to for direction. If you establish high levels of trust with each of your customers, when a potential new customer recognizes a need, and asks one of your existing customers, you'll get the new business.

Determine Alternatives and Options

Once a customer has recognized a need for something, and figured out who they think can help fill that need, they have arrived at step three of the Customer Buying Process. In this step they begin to wonder what choices they have. Choice has always been a really strong sales tool, and for good reason. The age old Good, Better, Best philosophy still works today because it's easy for customers to recognize these three alternatives.

Besides helping a customer establish Need Recognition, this third step in the Customer Buying Process is where the service writer becomes critically important in selling work. Your ability to educate the customer on what options they have will determine if they purchase from you, or not.

What alternatives and options might a customer have? Often we think of price point when it comes to options. Yes, this can be an option, but often there's really only one price available. The part is available at the same price from every vendor (at least the quality part you want to install is), and the labor is the labor. Much of the time there's no flexibility in what a repair, or service, will cost a customer. So what are the options?

Options can be:

- Do some of the repairs now, schedule others for later.

- Credit options through your credit program vendor.

- Convenience options – rental cars, shuttle rides, drop-off service, etc.

- Value options – lower quality parts, partial job, etc.

These options will appeal to different types of customers, in different situations. Maybe a customer just needs to get the vehicle running again, to sell it and just wants to fix the failed part, but not the oil leak that caused the part to fail. If the choice is ethical, you can offer it. If the choice is not ethical, then I encourage you to sell a complete repair.

There are times when breaking the total repair into multiple visits is the best thing to do. Take care of safety related issues now, and schedule appointments for the other issues in the future. This allows a customer to budget for the repairs, get everything taken care of over time, and for you to build an exceptional relationship with the customer which will likely lead to more business in the future – both theirs and those that they refer.

Many times, convenience is the primary motivation in whether a customer says yes to a repair or not. If you can make it convenient for the customer to be without their primary automobile, you'll often get the sale. A prime benefit of having customers drop the vehicle off when having it serviced is that they are far more likely to say yes to something you wish to sell them since you already have the automobile in the shop. Rides and shuttle service are great for some customers, but many others may prefer a rental vehicle or loaner car while their care is with you.

And lastly, sometimes money is the problem. Credit programs can help customers who really need to keep their vehicle on the road and don't have the money to do so. Don't be afraid to present your shop's credit program, or ask if the customer would like to apply. It can be a source of help for some customers. Just because you don't want another credit card, doesn't mean your customer isn't in a situation where they need the help.

Decision Making

If the first three steps of the Customer Buying Process all went well, the customer should now be at the point where they can make a decision. Keep in mind that the customer will not be able to make a decision if the first three steps have not been satisfied. If Need Recognition is not strong, or they do not have a firm grasp on exactly what Alternatives and Options are available, you will see hesitation in making a decision.

If you see hesitation in the customer after you've asked them for the sale, quickly assess if it is due to a lack of Need Recognition, or an incomplete understanding of the Alternatives and Options. Here are some feedback questions you can ask to determine which it may be:

- "Is it the time, or money, that concerns you?"

- "Would more information help?"

- "Would it help to know what other customers often ask me about this?"

- "Would it help to know what I'd do if it were my grandmother's car?"

- "Can I ask how you use the vehicle?"

Combining the use of these questions with the Mirroring technique from the Active Listening section will gain you enough information that you'll immediately know where you need to take the conversation. Sometimes it will be necessary to circle all the way back to the Need Recognition step and support stronger Need Recognition. Other times you'll discover that you didn't fully cover all the options that the customer was wondering, or was concerned, about.

Again, if the customer has strong Need Recognition and a good understanding of what their Alternatives and Options are, they will be in a position to make a decision at this stage.

Post-purchase Behavior

Once a decision has been made, there will always be some sort of post-purchase behavior. Behaviors that we want, and should encourage are:

- Leaving a positive review.

- Utilizing the shop's referral program.

- The customer feeling like they received value.

- A customer feeling safer and more confident in their automobile.

- A customer making their next appointment before leaving.

Behaviors that we do not want to happen:

- A customer changing their mind while sitting in the waiting area and surfing the internet.

- A customer leaving a negative review because they feel pressured into a sale, or that the value was not what it should have been (too expensive is what this will look like).

- A customer leaving and never returning.

- A customer returning due to a light still on (maintenance reminder lights are a common cause of customer dissatisfaction).

- A customer leaving without feeling they had their problem, or concern, resolved.

As a service writer, and shop, post-purchase behavior can be influenced through process, words, and actions. As a shop, you must have, and actively engage, a Quality Control Process. We address what this should look like later in the book, but know for now that ensuring quality workmanship goes a very long way in creating positive post-purchase behavior.

Other ways you can influence positive post-purchase behavior are:

- Remind customers how your Customer Referral Program works.

- Ask customers to leave a review.

- "Re-Sell" the job explaining to the customer the value they received today.

- Use words such as "You've made a great decision choosing these tires. By keeping them rotated regularly you can expect…"

- Constantly work on your selling skills, specifically around supporting the steps of Need Recognition and Determine Alternatives and Options.

Understanding the Customer Buying Process will go a long way in successfully selling every customer the service, maintenance, and repairs that they need. The most important thing to remember, besides knowing this information, is to always ask yourself "where in the Customer Buying Process is this customer right now". If you don't know the answer to that, ask one of the previously mentioned feedback questions to determine where they are.

Too often, service advisors will say to a customer something like "you need new brakes" and assume the customer recognizes the need and are then left shaking their head when the customer walks away without new brakes.

Another common scenario is for a customer to arrive at the shop for their oil change, and be presented a Courtesy Inspection with a long list of items they never knew they needed. When they are told they "need" something on this list, the customer, subconsciously, thinks "No. I don't. I just need the oil change" because this is the only thing they have Need Recognition of. Your ability to help create Need Recognition, as well as explain the Alternatives and Options, will be critical to your success selling.

We'll discuss the words you use to create Need Recognition coming up soon.

Accurate Estimates

Along with your communication skills, and knowing the Customer Buying Process, you must be able to write and explain estimates. To us, in the industry, this seems simple, yet to a customer estimates are viewed differently. The term "accurate estimate" may seem to be an oxymoron at times. In the automotive repair world, there is almost no such thing as an accurate estimate. There is a reason we call it an estimate! A price is suggested to a customer, and then the technician finds another problem or needed part during the repair. Although you may know that the problem or needed part could not have been anticipated, this can be very frustrating to customers and can lead to customers thinking that you're being dishonest, when you had no intention of being so.

Key Point

Like a gallon of milk, customers expect an automotive repair to be a set price. Be careful to not set cost expectations too soon in the repair process.

Most people inside the auto repair industry know that estimating repair costs has pitfalls and many times can't be as accurate as we'd all like it to be. Customers don't know this however. To a customer they are purchasing something that has a price, and they want to know what that price is! A good repair shop will learn to set customer expectations in such a way to avoid upsetting a customer over a repair estimate. The trick is to be as honest as you can be with the customer and impart some knowledge of what is involved in giving them an accurate estimate.

If you can't accurately estimate the cost, tell the customer up front! Explain to them what needs to occur before you can give them an accurate estimate. Explain to them that, without certain information, any estimate provided will likely have to be revised. Customers hate surprises, but if they know that there might be a surprise coming, at least they are prepared for it.

A common perception amongst service customers is that having their car repaired is expensive…and they're not always wrong! It can be expensive. Sometimes there's no getting around it. The only way that a repair shop can help with the perception of expense is to get good at estimating repair costs. More specifically, get good at not setting repair cost expectations too soon.

Something to Consider

Always explain to the customer what needs to happen in order to give them an accurate estimate of repair costs. Under promise and over deliver is a good policy!

The biggest estimating challenge might be in the creation of repair estimates (versus service or maintenance estimates). When a customer shows up at the door, nobody knows what might be wrong with the vehicle. Until a complete diagnostic can be performed on the problem, you won't have a good idea of what it will cost to repair the vehicle. Again, a service writer needs to remember not to jump to conclusions based on the customer description of the problem. Gather the appropriate information regarding the problem using a Customer Problem Analysis Sheet and let the technician make the diagnosis.

It is best to let the customer know that you won't have an idea of cost until after the technician takes a look at the vehicle. You may want to advise the customer that they will be responsible for one hour of diagnostic time. If the diagnostics look like they will take longer than an hour, the customer should be notified for their approval and an explanation given as to why it is taking longer than an hour. To err on the side of over communication will build a better customer experience.

Key Point

If diagnostics are consistently taking longer than the estimated amount of time you will need to find the root cause and address it.

Often times the cause is inadequate training, the wrong technician on the wrong job, or poor information collection.

If you find yourself in the situation where diagnostics are always taking longer than estimated, you will want to find the root cause. One of two things is generally happening. The overall knowledge level of your technicians may not be at an appropriate level, or the vehicle is not being given to a technician of the proper skill set. If you suspect that it is a knowledge issue then you will want to seek out and obtain good quality technical training for some, or all, of your technicians. There are a number of companies that offer such training for shops just like yours. (See Appendix H).

If you suspect that it is a work distribution problem, and you are a shop with a moderate number of technicians of varying skill level, put a written plan in place that allows for the vehicle to be handed up the skill chain after a certain amount of diagnostic time has elapsed. This will require the assistance of a shop foreman, or dispatcher, whose job it is to keep track of workflow in the shop. Some shops choose to not hand off the work, but to just get a shop foreman involved in the diagnostics more as a consultant. This is to not only get the vehicle diagnosed faster, but to help build the knowledge base of the technician working on the vehicle.

Key Point

A good shop foreman can help manage the learning and diagnostic capabilities of any shop.

When, in the course of your diagnostics, you find it necessary to take something significant apart, such as an engine, always obtain the customer's permission before doing so. When you can, during diagnostics, avoid putting the vehicle in a position where it can no longer be driven. If it is unavoidable that the customer's vehicle will not be able to be driven, let them know as soon as possible. When you do contact a customer to let them know their vehicle cannot be driven be sure to have a solution for them. This could be as simple as a offering loaner vehicle or providing a referral to a rental car agency. Never wait until the customer shows up to pick up their vehicle to let them know they won't be able to take it.

If the customer complaint is a MIL 'on' condition estimating gets even trickier. With MIL 'on' complaints there can be longer diagnostic times required depending on the DTC present and the skill set of the technician working on the problem. Many shops will charge the customer an automatic one hour diagnostic fee. In reality, DTC diagnostics can take far longer than just an hour to diagnose. Once again, I would advise letting the customer know if it looks like the diagnostics will take longer than the hour that they were told.

Something to Consider

Seek out and obtain the best quality technical training you can find for your technicians.

Repair estimating is a tricky business. Collecting information, letting the technicians do their job, and ensuring the customer feels listened to will all help in creating an accurate repair estimate. *Remember; never set a customer's expectation of what the repair is going to cost until a technician has looked at the vehicle.* Setting customer expectations in regards to cost of vehicle repair and then having to change that expectation is far more challenging than not setting the expectation in first place.

Customers will appreciate the honesty in taking this approach if the service writer explains to them what needs to happen for the shop to provide an accurate estimate.

Something to Consider

Don't be afraid to modify information collection forms like the Customer Problem Analysis Sheet in Appendix C to collect the information your technicians find most useful.

Service Maintenance Menus

Another tool that can help create a positive service experience for customers is the use of a maintenance menu. When customers bring their vehicle in for routine maintenance, having a service maintenance menu available for them to choose from can be a big help to both the service writer and the shop gross profits. Customers like seeing all the items laid out in front of them, and then having the option of choosing what they want to have performed. For many customers the ability to choose from a maintenance menu gives them a feeling of control over the transaction that might otherwise be lacking. This helps put the customer at ease, and can ultimately create higher revenues for the shop. The other benefit these menus carry is the that of "third-party affirmation". Seeing a third party (not you, not the customer) recommend a given service will sometimes allow the customer to feel that the recommendation is valid. This works in a variety of sales situations as well.

Even with this said, there seems to be a trend away from using maintenance menus in the selling process. Part of the trend stems from declining gross profit associated with maintenance services, the reduction in the number of required services for each mileage interval, the inclusion of manufacturer backed maintenance packages at the time of new car purchase, and the move to electronic information systems. The use of maintenance menus remains very important in terms of customer retention though.

Customer Satisfaction Point

Just like choosing food from a menu in a restaurant, customers love being able to pick their service offerings from a menu.

More progressive repair shops today keep the maintenance menu in front of the customer through the diligent, and sometimes creative, use of them, in all their forms, by the service advisor.

Combining the factory maintenance schedule from the Owner's Manual with an electronic menu board in the waiting room is a method of not only identifying what is recommended by the manufacturer at a given mileage (and letting the customer choose), but of breaking up these services into multiple repair visits. Many shops require the service advisor to identify to the customer each factory suggested maintenance interval and individual service. The customer is then given the option of having the entire service performed, or of breaking it into smaller operations possibly based on current monthly specials, or previous work performed. The development of electronic service management systems has made this even easier as some of these systems now link the published maintenance menu to the customer information in such a way that the information is only a mouse-click away. Many times the maintenance menu information can be shared via text or email as well – associated with the vehicle courtesy inspection.

```
Something to Consider

   Electronic menu boards have come a long way. They
are great not only for displaying common service items
but can be used for daily or seasonal specials as well.
```

If you are using an Electronic Menu Board the maintenance menu should include regular maintenance items commonly recommended at service intervals, as well as seasonal or monthly specials. Along with the recommended maintenance items, prices for each item should be included. The hesitation by some managers at this point is that prices can vary substantially from vehicle to vehicle. This leads them to not want to put a price and/or not include the item on an electronic board. Using language that states "starting at $xxx.yy" can help start the actual conversation. This is no different than any other advertising you've observed where the special price is $99.00 only to discover that the color you preferred and wanted to order is the regular price of $120.75. Customers understand variations and will be open to the conversation. Put a starting price on the electronic menu board and help your counter associates get better at selling!

Maintenance menus, in all their forms, allow a customer to not only hear what is recommended, but to see what is recommended and to see a price in writing. Choosing from a menu helps the customer feel empowered to make their own decisions about their vehicle, and allows the service writer an opportunity to customize the service experience.

Key Point

Service menus are a great way of building a long-term, sustainable relationship with your customers.

They serve to spread out repair costs, allow the opportunity to pre-schedule the next visit, and give the customer a feeling of control over what's being done to their vehicle.

Using a menu system can also help your repair shop in another way. It can help a customer spread out the cost of routine maintenance. By doing so, they are not as likely to be overwhelmed by an overly high bill at the time of their visit. They get to see everything that is needed for maintenance, choose what they want to spend money on now, budget for the next item, and the shop can make the next appointment during the current visit. This ultimately builds a consistent relationship with the repair shop. A consistent relationship means seeing your customer more often and creating a customer for life.

The Courtesy Inspection

A critical tool used for customer retention, customer education, and to increase shop revenue is the Courtesy Inspection (CI), or Multi-Point Inspection (MPI). These terms can be used interchangeably and refer to the vehicle inspection that is often performed as a free service to the customer. It also doesn't matter whether you're using electronic inspections, or paper inspections. The important thing is to perform vehicle inspections! All the inspection principles described here apply to either electronic inspections, or paper inspections.

Your customers rely on you and your employees to let them know what is going on with their automobile. A vehicle owner often has no way of knowing the true condition of their automobile. This is where offering a Courtesy Inspection as a valuable service to your customer can help to created that all-important *trust*. When used properly, this inspection becomes much like a report card to the customer, letting them know when everything is great, if something may need to be addressed soon, or when there is something that needs attention immediately.

Key Point

Courtesy Inspections are a very important tool in building customer trust, increasing customer retention, and improving overall shop revenue.

Courtesy Inspections are used by most repair shops. The problem is that these incredibly useful tools are too often used as a hammer to hit the customer over the head with (I'll describe how in a minute!). Customers have come to hate the sight of them, and repair shops have made them nothing more of a documentation tool. There is no reason for them not to be the best tool you have in educating a customer, or for them to be only documentation.

Courtesy Inspections are used as a hammer when they are only used to document the poor condition a vehicle is in.

Technicians, and their service consultants, are both guilty when it comes to improper inspection form use. Let's take the example of a customer who just purchased a relatively new car. The vehicle was well inspected, has fairly low mileage on it, and is not likely to need any service or repair work other than the oil change and tire rotation the customer has requested. Knowing this, both the advisor and the technician choose not to bother with performing the inspection (the tech sees this as a complete waste of time, and the advisor doesn't need anything else to do as they are already "too busy"). The customer pays for the work and leaves the shop having never been made aware of the free service that most customers are supposed to receive. This scenario then gets replayed the next four visits or so (approximately 20,000 miles). Never does the customer see a Courtesy Inspection sheet.

One day, the same customer comes in and the technician recognizes this vehicle may need some work (more likely they have suddenly recognized that a Courtesy Inspection might make them some money). Out comes the inspection form which is diligently filled out with everything this vehicle might possibly need. Here comes the hammer....

Something to Consider

When you use your Courtesy Inspection consistently not only will the customer get used to it, but they will never be surprised by a $2000 repair estimate, thus creating more trust.

The service advisor creates the estimate for everything the technician has identified and the customer is presented the fact that their vehicle suddenly (out of the blue in their mind) needs $1250 worth of work. The customer feels blindsided, and over time will learn to recognize that Courtesy Inspection as something that means bad things are about to get talked about (and most likely that they are about to get taken advantage of...in their mind). To protect themselves, because the customer is not sure if all this work is really needed, they say 'no thank you', pay for their oil change, and may never come back.

There is a better way.

The Better Courtesy Inspection

As with many things in life and business, the key to using this incredibly valuable tool is *consistency*. As human beings, we all love consistency. Consistency is essentially knowing what to expect. This is true whether it's going out to eat at a favorite restaurant, or hitting a home run because you know the pitch that's coming is a fastball. Consistency and Courtesy Inspections go together!

Let's take the same scenario from the last section, and instead of the technician and service advisor choosing to ignore the completion of the inspection, let's say they both recognize the importance of the tool. What they have observed through years of their experience, is that when they use it during every customer visit, no matter if the vehicle needs any work or not, the customer learns to expect it, and comes to trust what is on it. When the vehicle comes in for that very first oil change and tire rotation, the inspection form is filled out showing everything is in working order. There is no required work to be done, and nothing looks like it will need maintenance or repair before the next oil change or tire rotation. The customer is informed of this upon check out and is pleasantly surprised that a shop actually told her no work was needed. When the same scenario plays out over the next four visits she begins to get used to the fact that her vehicle is in good condition. Here comes the psychology....

On the first visit during which she receives a Courtesy Inspection that shows an item needs attention she recognizes this as out of the ordinary, and wants things returned to "normal". Since the inspection was performed consistently each visit, the needed repairs also are relatively small. She only needs $160 worth of work to make everything right again. The effect this has is that not only does she trust the shop to tell her nothing is needed, but trusts them when something *is* needed, and rarely will ever have a huge estimate when she's presented the inspection. Instead of a hammer, we've created a situation where there is a high level of trust and the customer will say yes to having the work done!

Same tool...two very different results.

Maximizing Your Courtesy Inspection

Here's the thing. Like most of the processes involved in automotive service, making the most out of your Courtesy Inspection doesn't sound that hard. And it isn't. The hard part is doing everything consistently and efficiently. To do so, takes attention, a little bit of work, and a lot of communication. If you want to implement an inspection program that is consistent, effective, and delivers satisfaction to your customer, there are some specific steps you can take.

Firstly, make sure you are using the right tool. By the right
tool, I mean an inspection form that works for exactly what
you want it to do. This can mean anything from a well-designed paper inspection form that both your technicians and
service consultants had input in designing, to an Electronic
Inspection Sheet (EIS) that not only allows for collection of
information, but allows pictures and videos to be texted to a
customer and the data used as a follow up tool.

I have no issues with shops continuing to use paper inspection forms if that is what works best for them. They do have
their limitations but they do not require much of a capital investment, are easy to find, and can be modified to suit whatever situation you may run into. Common challenges shops
will have with paper forms getting filled out include:

- Enough room for technicians to provide written
  notes.

- Too many, or too few, inspections items.

- Easily dirtied.

- Technicians "pencil whipping" the form.

- Technicians "cherry picking" the work they want to
  do on the customer's car.

- Must be acquired in at least duplicate, if not triplicate, if the form is to be used for follow-up.

- More difficult to modify than electronic.

These challenges can be overcome with enough attention to detail. Regular meetings to communicate with technicians about how the form is working for them, why you are using the form to begin with, and how the process can be improved with help with technicians consistently filling them out, and filling them out correctly. If communication is poor, you will end up with the previously described "hammer" scenario.

Generally, you will want a form that can address somewhere between 25 and 30 items, have enough room for technicians to write notes, and be able to document any vehicle damage. The shorter the form, the more room for notes you will need. The popular red, yellow, green check box format is well understood by both service personnel and customers.

Key Point

Watch the Courtesy Inspection video on the Repair Shop Rescue YouTube channel for a great discussion on maximizing the results of your Courtesy Inspections.

If you need to address the challenges of "cherry picking" (only recommending easy, or good paying work) or "pencil whipping" (drawing a continuous line through jus the 'green is good' boxes) you will need to establish better communication with the technicians. Many technicians do not recognize the benefit of a consistent inspection process. Often they only see them as a piece of paper and more "needless" work. If the discussion is had that explains why you do these inspections (to create and build trust with customers), where the technicians will see the benefit (in their wallet when the work gets sold), and feedback is given regularly when a technician does a good job (to reinforce the fact that they are making more money) then the paper forms, and program in general can be successful.

Key Point

Regular meetings where you discuss your inspection program with you technicians can not only help improve the program, but it can help them understand the benefits of having the program!

The second piece to maximizing the use of a courtesy inspection is making a proper introduction to the program to the customer. There are many reasons for formally introducing the customer to your program, but I think the primary benefit is in your customer's understanding of why you do it. You want the customer to understand that this is a free service you provide all of your customers because as an organization you believe that it is your responsibility to let the customer know the condition of the operating systems of the vehicle. You also want to get the customer use to having this done each time they come in. You can avoid any miscommunication when the customer comes in for a tire rotation and sees their hood open by communicating what you do and why you do it. Should a customer wish to opt out, they should be able to do so with a signature saying so. Otherwise I suggest having a shorter form available that just addresses easily viewed systems. Remember, the program is for their benefit and should be communicated at such. Putting such a statement, or description on your website and at the service counter, will help communicate the program to your customers (and possibly remind other employees of why you have the program).

You may hear technicians suggest they should get paid for doing the inspections. Some shops do pay their technicians between 0.3 and 0.5 hours for each inspection. However, based on many years of experience, it is generally not required that they be paid to perform these inspections. The theory is that most of the inspection can be done while other work is being accomplished, and that the payment comes in form of upsells (the advisor selling the work the technician recommends). If technicians are paid to do inspections, you often find the same problems as when they are not paid: not enough forms completed, not completing the forms fully, and the same "pencil whip" and "cherry pick" challenges. A shorter form, room for notes, and regular reminders to follow the process are a better solution than paying to perform.

The above advice is valid for an Electronic Inspection Program as well.

Electronic Inspections (EIS or DVI)

The last few years have seen the proliferation of EIS. Many shops who were the first to adopt the process, and software, found that the inspections took just as long to perform, suffered from the same "cherry picking" challenges, and often were a bit more difficult to implement. As time went on however, and individuals began to get used to using the system, software improved, and the benefits of texting, or emailing, pictures and videos became apparent EIS began to really catch on.

Today, there are still challenges in fully implementing EIS in a manner that makes efficient use of both the technician's time and improves service counter workflow, but this is being improved almost daily by the software companies.

Often, the EIS associated with any given service management system is either not customizable enough, or is not compatible with email or texting platforms and thus is difficult to share with all customers. The standalone EIS software does a great job of being customizable but often cannot be integrated enough with the current service management system to avoid duplication of work at the service counter (transferring of notes, recommendations, etc.). These shortcomings are not present in 100% of systems and will get better with each passing month as the industry rapidly adapts to the technology and the software improves.

When adopting EIS for your shop it is important to maintain a high level of communication with the users of the hardware and software. The capital expense, and maintenance expense for that matter, that will be incurred to implement an EIS program is not light for many shops. Therefore, you will want to make sure that technicians and service advisors find the software relatively intuitive and the hardware easy to use. Be sure to understand what platform and hardware the software works best on (and listen to the recommendations!), demo the software with enough of your technicians and service advisors that it can be fully evaluated. There is no one software platform that does it all right now, although there are many that do a good job with just inspections.

The time to adoption of any EIS program will depend on how deeply you want to connect the software with your current processes. Some shops have taken it to the level of electronic dispatch and customer marketing, while others have kept it at a level where it is only used for courtesy inspections. No matter how you choose to use EIS, there will be a learning curve.

Something to Consider

Not everyone will be excited to implement EIS, but once they see the customer end of it, they instantly recognize the benefit of the program.

The great thing about EIS is the ease with which you can adopt, and modify, multiple inspection forms to be used as Quick Inspections (if a customer doesn't have time for a full inspection), your regular Courtesy Inspection, an Alignment Pre-Check, Brake Inspection, or any other inspection you could imagine. All the forms reside right there on the phone or tablet. The inclusion of pictures and video in these inspections makes selling even easier as now these inspection forms are just as effective when the customer is back at the office, at home, or anywhere else for that matter! The form gets emailed or texted, the customers opens up the link and can see the pictures while the advisor describes what needs to be done and why. The forms are then stored to be used in follow marketing for customers who choose not to have the worked performed.

Due to the customer satisfaction and marketing benefits of Electronic Courtesy Inspections, I encourage all shops to begin the adaptation process. By the time you read this, many systems will have EIS that can fully integrate with the dispatch process, marketing processes, and improved customer communication systems.

Whether you choose to utilize EIS, or just paper, your Courtesy Inspection program is a crucial piece to growing business, improving customer retention, and increasing revenue. Pay close attention to the process from customer introduction, to technician communication, to customer follow up and it will pay dividends for you and your shop.

Introducing the Courtesy Inspection

In my opinion, an important part of your sales process at the service counter should be to always introduce your Courtesy Inspection. This means reminding the customer of why you perform these inspections, how often they can expect to have one done, and what it looks like. Even if you're using digital inspections, you can have a printed screen grab of a great inspection laminated and present on the service counter.

Using a word track to introduce the inspection, can keep customers from being upset that they see their hood open when they just stopped by for a tire rotation. A word track such as this is very effective:

"As I'm sure you remember, because we at XYZ Automotive believe it is part of our responsibility to help you ensure the safety, reliability, and fuel economy of your vehicle, we offer every customer, every visit, a free vehicle inspection."

This word track can even be printed poster sized and used as marketing inside your customer waiting area. Over time, customers will begin to see your inspection not as a sales tool, but as evidence they do a great job maintaining their vehicle.

The Words You Use When Selling Matter

When you are talking to a customer about what their vehicle needs, the words you use really do matter. We've spent some time exploring the Customer Buying Process, but to ensure the customer is fully engaged, and moving through the process as you need them to, using the right words is crucial.

For example, let's look at an example word track for a needed repair:

> "Mr. Allan? Can I show you something the technician working on your vehicle called to my attention? I think you'll find it interesting." At this point, you would hand Mr. Allan a pair of safety glasses and walk out to the service bay. "When he went to drain your engine oil for the oil change, he discovered that very little came out. Check out this oil leak: Here is your transmission, and this, of course, is your engine. Notice how the oil leak only appears on this lower section of what we call the bell housing, with some dripping appearing right here?" You would point at the torque converter inspection cover, where you note

a little oil. "Because of where the oil is appearing, we know that there are only two possible places from which fluids could be leaking: the rear main seal at the crankshaft and the front pump seal of the transmission. Based on the fact that your engine oil was significantly low, and by the color and consistency of the dripping fluid, we feel confident that it is the rear main oil seal that is leaking. Can we go ahead and return that to factory condition for you?"

You'd finish by talking the customer through the time and expense of the repair, as well as potentially giving them choices as able.

Note that there are several things there that help the service counter employee make the sale:

- The customer clearly sees the problem with their own eyes. If the customer is not present, then pictures and video are absolutely necessary. We've arrived at a time when we can sell just as easily over the phone as we can in person if we use the technology available to us.
- The customer is educated both on why the repair is needed and where. You can also use your animated sales tools here, such as MotoVisuals, to demonstrate to the customer, present or not, what the rear main seal does and what happens when it leaks.
- The customer is given options and clear cost and time expectations are communicated.

Are there ways that word track could be tailored to fit your needs? Sure! Just keep in mind the different customer types, the buying process, and use the tools available at your disposal (whether educational and visual resources or multi-point inspections, etc) to your advantage.

Here's a scenario where the customer may have come in for an oil change, and your technician noticed the vehicle needs front brakes.

There are two really important things to do here. The first is to reinforce with the customer that they do a great job maintain their automobile, and the second is to begin to establish the process of Need Recognition. Begin by showing the customer the Courtesy Inspection and saying:

"As usual you're doing a great job maintain your automobile – check out everything here in green."

Even if the customer doesn't really do a great job maintain their automobile, statistically, it's likely there'll still be more green checked off on the sheet, than things needing attention. This word track gets the customer to begin believing that they are someone who does a great job maintaining their automobile. Next you need to begin establishing Need Recognition. To do this start by saying:

"Your technician has only noted one area of concern. You may have noticed a grinding or sandy type noise when slowing to a stop?"

Or you could say:

"I don't remember if you mentioned a noise when stepping on the brake pedal..."

Follow either of these word tracks with:

"The noise is due to the brake pad friction material being completely worn out. Would you like to see for yourself?"

Or:

"I can show you what's causing that noise if you'd like to see?"

The same can be done over the phone with today's technology. If the customer is looking at a copy of the inspection, and a picture, or video, of the problem, these same words will work.

You'll then want to lead into your selling conversation. At this point you should have established Need Recognition and the customer should be ready, or curious about, hearing the options and alternatives. The next question to ask:

"Can I ask how you use the vehicle on a regular basis?"

This starts a very important conversation where you'll be using Active Listening, a concept called "Use no to get a yes", and mirroring. When the customer answers this question you will understand what may be important to them. For instance:

Customer: "Mostly commuting to work and then up to camp on the weekends."

Now the service writer can use mirroring to get a little more information, or reinforce what they think might be important to the customer.

Service Writer: "Camp on weekends?"

Customer: "Yeah, me and my wife love spending time in the mountains just to get away every week."

Now you've set the customer up for the "use no to get a yes" technique. Customers really want to say no to being sold something, yet this technique allows them to say no, yet is essentially a 'yes'. It's a play on words – nothing devious!

Service Writer: "So would it be crazy of me to think that it's important to you to have your brakes in factory level operating condition at all times?"

The customer should respond with "No! That's not crazy at all!"

Now you can ask for the sale:

Service Writer: "Then can I go ahead and have your technician return your brakes to factory level operating condition so you know you'll safely get to camp and back every weekend?"

Of course, if the customer has Need Recognition, and understands their Alternatives and Options, they will say 'yes' at this point. The exact same strategy can be used to sell batteries as well.

Let's take another look at an example word track for a malfunction indicator lamp (check engine light) repair:

> "Mr./Ms. Customer, the diagnostic specialist I've had looking at your vehicle has identified the cause of your check engine light as a bad oxygen sensor. He would like permission to go ahead and replace that component. Parts and labor will cost you (insert price). I want you to be aware that although I have confidence in his diagnosis, the challenge with oxygen sensors is that they are critical components in the testing of other engine control systems. Once the system has identified a problem with the oxygen sensor it actually suspends all the other tests it would

normally conduct on the other engine control systems. This means that once we fix the current oxygen sensor problem that we know exists currently, and the system can then run its normal complement of tests it may find other problems that will then cause the light to come on again. We will do our best to get your vehicle to run its other tests while it is here so that, should it find something else, you won't have to make a second trip for diagnosis and service, but I wanted to make you aware of the chance that the system will find something else. Can we go ahead and replace the faulty oxygen sensor?"

You'd then explain what that would cost and what timelines might look like, expanding the potential cost and timeline as needed if other problems arise.

As we discussed earlier in our needed repairs example, there are several things there that help the service writer lead up to the sales ask:

- The customer clearly sees the problem with their own eyes.
- The customer is educated both on why the repair is needed and where.
- The customer is given options and clear cost and time expectations are communicated.

Preventative maintenance relies on trust and education perhaps more than any other type of sale. If you or your sales counter staff can create the Need Recognition for your customer, that also goes a long way—even if you are only setting the customer up for a multi-visit sell. Educational tools are also incredibly helpful when it comes to selling preventative maintenance.

Consider the following word track as a starting point:

> "Mr./Ms. Customer, I was looking at the preventative maintenance list (insert manufacturer) published for your (insert model) and I see from your service history with us that you are due for (insert single item or multiple items). Because I know you use this vehicle for work you might consider having this/these item(s) performed while we have your vehicle here for your oil change. Doing so will help ensure uninterrupted use of your vehicle."

The Power of a Signature

After the customer has told the service writer what their concerns are or what the maintenance request is, and have filled out the Customer Problem Analysis Sheet with the writer, your service writers should then print the repair order (if you are still printing repair orders), have the customer read it over to make sure they didn't miss anything, and then have the customer sign the repair order. If you are a paperless shop, have the customer sign the repair order electronically using your signature pad.

A signature on the repair order does a couple of things. Firstly, from a legal perspective, it helps protect the shop, the technician, and the service writer from misunderstandings. If a signature is not collected, the customer can suggest that they were not aware of what services were to be performed. With a signature on the repair order, it's much harder for the customer to claim the shop did not have authorization to operate, or perform, work on their vehicle.

Secondly, when someone signs a document they have more commitment and buy-in to the process. This can further help the customer feel like they are more a part of the repair or service process. By signing the document, the customer acknowledges the repairs that are to be performed, and expects the shop to operate the vehicle during the course of diagnosis and repair.

Vehicle Delivery Process

The last, and often overlooked part of the customer experience is the vehicle delivery process. This is where the vehicle is returned to the customer. This is the part of the service counter workflow where you can influence the last step of the Customer Buying process – Post-purchase Behavior.

Customer Satisfaction Point

Always remind the customer of the value they've received in choosing to have you do the work today. "Mr. Smith, you've made a great choice with these tires today" can go a long way in positively influencing the customer's post-purchase behavior.

Many times repair shops view this transaction as "collecting money", or for problem vehicles, "getting the car out of here." The customer views things very differently of course!

Something to Consider

Schedule the customer's next service visit at the time of delivery. This allows the customer to know what to expect for the next service or repair and allows you to ensure the customer will be returning to you!

From the customer's perspective the vehicle delivery is the culminating event in the service process. They are looking for a justification for spending money and want to be assured that the vehicle has been repaired. The delivery process should start with a thorough review of the customer invoice between the service writer and the customer. The goal is to make sure that the customer understands what each operation was, why it was necessary, and what the associated expense was. This is when the relationship with the customer becomes fully developed.

Time spent making sure the customer understands the work performed will result in long-term benefits to the repair shop. As the service writer builds trust with each customer, this process becomes less time consuming. Take the time to explain every line of the invoice in detail even when you're busy – if this is what the customer type requires. If you're dealing with a Quadrant I customer type, you will not need to explain every line, but restating the value received is always a good idea.

Customer Satisfaction Point

Whenever possible, help the customer find where the vehicle has been parked. If snow is present, delivering the vehicle to the doorstep is a great practice.

Remember, unlike purchasing consumer goods, the customer is spending hard-earned money on something that they may not see tangible results in. Understanding each item on the repair order, and why it was necessary will go a long way in helping the customer to perceive value in their service purchase. This is especially true when explaining necessary maintenance items. If you previously used the maintenance menu to sell the customer maintenance service, you'll find it to be much less time consuming at this point as they've already developed an understanding of what was needed and why.

This is also a great time to talk to the customer about future scheduled maintenance, previously prioritized repairs, and to schedule the next appointment. When the customer has given their vehicle up to you for the day they are expecting to have the shop try to sell them something and may be very defensive about it. By being proactive and "selling" the customer the next service, or reminding them of the next priority in what needs to be repaired, at the time of delivery, they don't necessarily equate the transaction with being sold something. The customer sees it as more of a "heads-up" on what will need to be done next. This gives them time to process the information, make decisions, ask questions, and budget for the maintenance or repair. Doing so can help significantly in building a solid relationship with the customer because the customer feels more in control of the next transaction.

Customer Satisfaction Point

Paying attention, and following through, on every last detail of the service experience will create customers for life.

Once payment is received, it is advisable to walk the customer to the parking lot and make sure they can easily find their vehicle. If you have a small parking lot, and it will be obvious to the customer where their vehicle is parked, this may not be entirely necessary, but it does send the message that you care about the customer and their convenience. Numbering the parking spaces in a location that is easy to identify and having the technician report which space the vehicle is parked in is another solution often used to help customers locate their vehicle in larger parking lots.

In metro areas where customer vehicles are parked on the street after service, it is even more important that the service writer help the customer find the vehicle. The last thing you want is for a technician to have parked the vehicle somewhere around the block where it takes the customer a long time to find the vehicle. The customer may just get in their car, drive off, and never return for service because they are disgruntled about the inconvenience. You will never know why they didn't return to you for service. Insisting on the service writer bringing the customer to the car, or the car to the customer will avoid any potential for losing a customer over something so simple.

Customer Satisfaction Point

Always remove the paper floor mats and other protective covers from the vehicle before returning it to the customer.

Having to dispose of this trash may undo any goodwill you've created by using it in the first place.

One other alternative to the service writer physically delivering the vehicle is to hire someone whose job it is to retrieve customer's vehicles during the times of day when customers are picking up vehicles. During other times of day they can be helping to clean the premises, perform facility maintenance, or train for a future position as technician or service writer.

If you are in an area of the country where snow is common, and you have the personnel, it's always nice to have the vehicle delivered to the door for the customer. Customers appreciate the extra attention, and the increased convenience.

A Final Word on Delivery

Even if all of the service processes went well and the customer appears comfortable with the final bill, all the goodwill created can be undone if the customer gets in their vehicle and finds a warning light on, a greasy handprint, or the radio stations no longer preset.

This is where customer satisfaction is the responsibility of the entire service department. Seat covers, steering wheel covers, and floor mats should be made available to technicians. Technicians and service writers need to be encouraged to work together to ensure that these protections are put in place during the time the vehicle is in service. While these protections should be used during the service visit, they should likewise be removed from the vehicle before the customer picks the vehicle up.

Occasionally I come across someone who thinks that it's good to leave the paper floor mat in a vehicle so the "customer knows we took measures to protect their vehicle". However, think of it like a customer: what will a customer do with the floor mat? Now they have to dispose of it. Or it stays in the vehicle, gets wet and is soon destroyed. It is good practice to remove all protective covers from the vehicle before the customer picks the vehicle up. Try to make the customer feel as though nobody else was ever in their vehicle.

The radio is major pitfall resulting in an annoyed customer. Technicians should never change a customer's radio station, or adjust the volume. During repair work it is best to just turn the radio off.

There are times when during an extended test drive a technician may want to listen to the radio, and this is acceptable if the technician remembers to return the radio to the station previously programmed. Radio station presets should be recorded on the repair order before work is performed on the vehicle in the event that battery power must be disconnected during vehicle service. Some service facilities ask that service writers record radio station presets at the time they collect vehicle information. This may or may not be practical depending on your service facility and write-up process, but is something that should be considered.

Something to Consider

Have your service writers record radio station presets
at the time of initial write up.

Our vehicles are important to us and are an extension of who we are. Any abnormality we notice when we get into our car after service feels like a violation to us. You can help to ensure a positive customer experience by encouraging all of the shop's employees to create a good experience for your customer. It's many little things that add up to a positive service visit, but it can be just one negative that brings the whole experience down.

Vehicle Delivery is the last chance you have to complete the sales cycle by asking the customer leave a positive review, or to contact you if they feel for any reason they cannot leave a positive review. I encourage everyone to remind each customer of the shop's customer referral program at this time as well.

Paying attention to how the customer gets their vehicle back can solidify the customer's positive experience, further build customer trust, and ensure future business.

Always Remember

- **A successful repair experience begins with a proper scheduling process.**
- **Greeting customers in a positive manner sets a tone for everyone waiting for service.**
- **Practice active listening with each customer.**
- **Ensure service writers are diligent about collecting information from customers regarding the concern.**
- **Utilize a Customer Problem Analysis Sheet.**
- **Accurate estimating is about setting customer expectations. Don't give a customer a repair estimate until after the technician has had the opportunity to diagnose the vehicle.**
- **Utilize service maintenance menus to help the customer feel empowered and to pre-schedule future appointments.**

Chapter 3: Communication

In This Chapter

- **Service writer communication with technicians.**
- **Communication with customers.**
- **Handling challenging customers.**

There are many times during the service process where communication is important. Communication between customers and repair shop employees, service writers and technicians, and shop management and employees contribute to the customer's perception of their service experience. Every shop owner and manager who wants to improve profits will pay attention to communication. In this chapter we focus on communication between technicians and service writers, and how to handle challenging customers.

Service Desk Communication

One important aspect of the service write-up and delivery process that we have only touched on briefly is the importance of communication between the service writer and the technician. Each individual, whether a service writer or a technician, has an idea of the type of information that he or she deems important to successfully diagnosing and repairing a vehicle, yet the types of information don't always coincide.

Technicians and service writers must develop a mutual respect for each other. They must rely on each other in order to successfully diagnose and repair customer concerns. Although a business owner or manager can't always smooth differences in personalities, they can put processes in place that encourage good communication between service writers and technicians.

Key Point

Service writers need to collect information regarding the customer concern and let the technicians do their job. Beware the temptation to diagnose the vehicle at the time of write up.

To resolve some of the challenges of communication between writers and technicians you can start by asking that the technician bring the service writer to the vehicle and show them exactly what the problem looks like while explaining what caused it. We all learn differently, and come from different experiential backgrounds. Some service writers can understand a problem, or solution, just from a verbal or written description, but others need to see it.

Key Point

Utilize a Customer Problem Analysis sheet to help quantify the customer concern. See Appendix C.

Showing the service writer the problem gives the writer a chance to see the problem for themselves, ask questions regarding the problem and solution, and allows them to better explain to the customer what needs to be done and why. Doing so also helps to increase the service writer's knowledge base regarding common repairs.

From the technician's perspective, they want information regarding what the customer concern is, what they have to do to make the problem manifest, and maybe how long it's been going on. The one thing a technician doesn't want to be told is what the problem might be. Like detectives, technicians are trained to see the problem themselves, analyze symptoms, and run tests to come up with a solution. Often times telling a technician what a problem is, or guessing at a cause, will only create more problems and worse, may create more communication challenges within the shop.

Utilizing a Customer Problem Analysis Sheet can help gather information for diagnosis without the service writer interjecting what he or she thinks the problem is. Service writers should be encouraged to just ask questions, and gather information. The temptation to "diagnose on the drive", or give the customer an estimate as to what the problem likely is, and how much it will cost to fix, can often backfire if done without a proper diagnosis.

Something to Consider

Encourage your technicians to speak with customers. It can go a long way towards helping a customer develop a relationship with your shop.

I strongly recommend holding regular shop meetings to discuss communication between service writers and technicians. Putting the two in a room together, with a specific agenda, and in a well-controlled environment can keep problems from growing, nip certain challenges in the bud, and create an atmosphere of teamwork. Holding regular shop meetings with the technicians and service writers to discuss the collection of information and communication between the two parties can stop communication problems before they begin to affect the customer experience.

Technicians and Customers

There is another area of communication that I think is often neglected – communication between customers and technicians. Communication between a customer and a technician can pay big dividends for a repair shop. Technicians at times are removed from contact with the customer. This can some-times be a good thing, but can also be a source of frustration for the customer, as well as create a gap in communication that affects the repair. Some customers would like to speak with the technician who is working on their vehicle, or at the very least, know who is working on their vehicle. To other customers it doesn't matter who is working on their vehicle as long as their concerns are resolved.

Customer Satisfaction Point

Establish expectations for how your technicians are to appear in uniform. Shirts tucked in and boots laced should be the minimum expectation.

In either event, I've always encouraged technicians to speak with shop customers. This personal connection can often help develop the relationship between the customer and the repair shop. In speaking with customers I often hear the words "my mechanic" spoken proudly. I've been telling technicians for a long time that it's possible to create their own business within a business by speaking with customers themselves. Years ago when I was a technician in a multi-technician shop, I would go out of my way to speak with my customers. By doing so I had many customers request that only I work on their vehicle. This created plenty of work for me, made it easier for the ser-vice writer to up-sell because of the trust I'd built with the customer, and helped build the relationship between the cus-tomer and the service center. Granted, this doesn't work with every technician, but if you've got technicians who are good with customers use them to reduce the load on your service writers and build the relationship between your shop and your customer.

If you agree that having the technician speak to the customer is a good idea then discuss this with your technicians. Explain to them why you think it's a good idea, listen to their opinion, and try to create a process where they are comfortable speaking with the customer. Be conscious, however, of the amount of time it may take out of the technician's day to speak with a customer.

If you're going to suggest that your technicians speak with your customers, take steps to ensure the technicians look presentable to the customer. It's impossible to stay spotless as a technician, but little things like having shoes and boots laced up, and shirts tucked in can go a long way in making your technician look presentable to a customer! Technicians should also never smoke in front of a customer. Establish expectations for how your technicians are to present themselves and be sure to maintain those expectations.

Remember

Active Listening:

1. Eye Contact

2. Head Nodding

3. Reflection

You may have a technician or two who is not comfortable speaking with customers and that's okay too. If this is the case, then the communication between the service writer and technician is critical. As mentioned previously, the service writer must translate customer language into technician language and vice versa. Be sure to use a Customer Problem Analysis Sheet to collect the facts regarding the customer's concern. This helps to ensure information the technician perceives as useful gets collected along with information that the customer and service writer think will be useful to the technician.

By encouraging good communication between service writers and technicians you can increase the efficiency of your repair facility, increase customer satisfaction, and create a pleasant working environment. Give your service writers, and your technicians, tools such as regular meetings, checklists, or communication devices to create stronger communication between them. Doing so will create positive results throughout your organization.

How to Handle Challenging Customers

Challenging customers come in all forms from angry and verbally abusive, to passively aggressive people. Usually these customers came to be of the mind they are in for a reason. Granted, there are some customers who just seem to revel in being cantankerous, but for the most part upset customers have a reason to be upset.

There is generally a small percentage of customers in every business who you will never be able to please. The mistake that many of us make is to focus on this small percentage of customers. Don't let a small percentage of customers who are irascible taint your view of every customer that comes through the door. In general customers are very pleasant to deal with.

When you find yourself having to deal with a disgruntled customer, remembering a few simple techniques can help to diffuse the situation. Both parties being upset and defensive won't amount to anything positive for the customer or your repair shop.

In my work as a manufacturer representative it was my job to deal with extremely unhappy customers. Over *years of dealing with these customers I came to the realization that in virtually every case of an unhappy customer, all that was needed to resolve the customer concern was to listen to the customer.* That's all! Virtually every one of the irate customers I dealt with either felt they weren't being listened to, or actually weren't being listened to, as evidenced by their repair history.

No, the customer isn't always right, but it's not always okay to tell them that! Sometimes you have to act as though they are right. Active listening, expressing empathy, and relating to how the customer is feeling can be incredibly helpful. Try to put yourself in the customer's position or frame of mind (no matter how difficult that may be!).

Active listening is the first tool that a seasoned service writer uses when communicating with challenging customers. Active listening includes making eye contact, nodding your head in agreement, clarifying what you are hearing the customer say, and essentially engaging in the conversation, in a positive manner, with the customer. Remember that most customers get upset with repair shops because they don't feel like they are being heard or they don't perceive that their concerns are being addressed.

Key Point

Don't focus on the small percentage of customers who are difficult to please. Remember that the majority of your customers are pleasant to deal with and are pleased with your services.

Sometimes expressing empathy can help the situation. Just saying something like: "I imagine that you feel frustrated because you've had to return for your MIL 'on' condition again" can go a long way in helping a customer feel like they are being heard. It won't make the problem go away, but at least they feel validated that they are upset and that it's okay (whether you really think it's okay for them to be upset or not).

Other times, relating a similar experience you once had with what the customer is experiencing can help the customer feel like they have a "friend" in the shop. Don't pretend that it's the same problem or that because it was no big deal to you it should be nothing for the customer to be upset about. Instead use it as a form of empathy. "I know how you might be feeling…I once had a similar experience in XYZ and boy was it ever frustrating!" Again, this validates the customer's feelings and creates a situation where real dialogue can happen.

Once you have been able to establish some rapport with a challenging customer, and have listened to everything that they have to say, by using active listening techniques and empathy, you can then find a mutually agreeable resolution to the problem. Don't make excuses for shoddy workmanship, or an improper repair. Doing so *sounds* like you are making excuses and the customer can see right through them.

Customer Satisfaction Point

Always avoid patronizing a customer. Never make excuses as to why a situation occurred.

Tell the customer what you can do to help the situation. It could be engaging the customer in a test drive to better understand the complaint, admitting that the shop made a mistake, and putting a technician on the vehicle right away to correct the mistake, or if possible, offering the customer a ride, a loaner vehicle, or a rental car while you resolve the concern.

In the case of a repair that was completed by "taking your best guess" it can be very challenging to calm a customer down. The best way of handling this situation is to avoid it to begin with. When it comes to a repair where there is no obvious solution to the problem (usually due to diagnostic equipment limitations, technician skill restraints, or occasionally time restraints) it is best to be upfront about this with the customer. The phrase "what we've seen work in the past" can help a customer feel better about the fact that you are really guessing at what repair will resolve the complaint.

I further suggest explaining to the customer that this repair solution is your best attempt at resolving the concern. Explain to the customer what the next options will be if this solution does not work. Along with the options, explain the reasons why you are choosing the repair route that you are, as well as what the next options are likely to cost. This will set the customer expectation that you are truly trying your best to resolve their concern and provide them with the lowest cost solution that will result in the complaint being taken care of.

Something to Consider

Avoid "guessing" at the cause of a customer concern. Doing so can lead to a very upset customer.

You can't make everyone happy, but you can provide most people with a pleasant experience. Many of us have worked in the automotive industry so long that we've forgotten what it was like to bring our vehicle to someone else to have any work done on it. Try taking your car to another service facility, one where you don't know anyone, and have a minor repair or maintenance service performed on it. Experience for yourself what your customer might go through. This will help to keep the customer experience forefront in your mind. Have your employees do the same.

Knowing what your competition is doing pays dividends in other ways too. It can help you to set yourself apart by creating a business atmosphere, or service experience, that is different than what other shops do. I speak with many repair shops who tell me that knowing what other shops in their area are doing has helped them to treat their customers differently. All of these shops have been growing at steady rates for a number of years!

Key Point

Keep perspective by taking your own vehicle to other repair shops for service. This will help you understand what customers experience in the marketplace.

Keeping perspective when it comes to the customer experience will help you to create a positive customer experience and maintain a solid core of customers. Make sure you know what your shop is doing that is like what others are doing. Also understand how it may be different from what others are doing. Learning to handle challenging customers will build respect for your organization and ultimately result in higher customer retention numbers for your repair shop.

Shop Meetings

The last communication tool that I want to mention is shop meetings. I strongly recommend holding regular shop meetings to encourage communication between service writers and technicians. Here's the problem – everyone hates shop meetings! They hate shop meetings because too often they are only held to resolve some sort of an issue. Holding regularly scheduled meetings allows for better communication, resolution of potential issues (before they become and issue), and shorter meetings.

Here are my rules for holding shop meetings:

1. **Keep it short. 15 to 20 minutes is enough if they are held regularly.**
2. **Have an agenda for each meeting.**
3. **Consistency – weekly is what I recommend although monthly and quarterly is okay.**

Putting service advisors and technicians in a room together, with a specific agenda, and in a well-controlled environment can keep problems from growing, nip certain challenges in the bud, and create an atmosphere of teamwork. Holding regular shop meetings with the technicians and service writers to discuss the collection of information and communication between the two parties can stop communication problems before they begin to affect the customer experience.

Consistency in holding shop meetings allows for the meetings to stay short. Having an agenda gives everyone the idea that we're not just here for a "gripe session".

At some point if you've held these meetings consistently, you may run out of ideas for the agenda. What tends to happen is that, at first, you've got all kinds of things to talk about, but as time goes on and the organization becomes more and more fine tuned the ideas wane. This is where keeping a notebook to track meeting ideas is useful. You can also introduce topics by using short training videos on a topic and then have a group discussion on how to implement the topic in your organization.

Meeting Topics can include:

- Courtesy Inspections.
- Production goals.
- Customer referral program initiatives.
- Upcoming marketing.
- Employee referral programs.
- Shop workflow.
- Service Counter workflow.
- Operating hours.
- Work schedules.
- Quality Control processes.
- Tool and equipment needs.
- Training.
- Videos that can be found at https://www.youtube.com/c/GregMarchandRepair-ShopRescueCoach

When to hold shop meetings can be a challenge as well. I like to hold meetings early in the week, so that if there's things to be worked on, or changed, we have the week to do it. Mondays however are terrible days to have a shop meeting. Most of my coaching clients choose to hold them on Tuesday. Next you need to decide on a time. After the workday is done is a miserable time to have meetings – everyone wants to go home! I suggest holding meetings first thing in the morning.

Require everyone to come to work 30 minutes early every Tuesday. It will be a regularly scheduled day, pay them each an extra half-hour to be there, and be consistent with it. Make it a condition of employment, just like attending training classes. By holding the meeting in the morning, before you open, you have an automatic hard stop to the meeting. Yes, you may have to deal with the "I need to drop the dog off at doggy daycare" situation, but generally parents of kids, or pets, can figure this out once a week if it's a condition of employment. Don't allow any excuses for employees to get out of these regular meetings.

If you would rather hold meetings at lunch, I don't hate the idea. Lunchtime also has a built-in stop time, but the phones don't stop ringing. When employees come and go from the meetings, it disrupts the meeting cadence and slows any progress.

Communication Summary

Communication within your organization, as well as communication outside your organization is very important to your success, and the success of the shop. Communication will include verbal, and non-verbal (body language) forms. Learning to communicate well is an aspect of managing a repair shop, or working a service counter that everyone can get better at.

No matter what communication form you are engaging with, practice is important. It's hard to just read something on these pages and incorporate it into your day. Intentional practice with specific forms of communication will help you to get good, if not great, at all of them. Take one form of communication each week and work on it. Make it your mission this week, or month, to get really good at Active Listening. Then, the next month, get good at introducing your Courtesy Inspection.

Focused attention on learning and practicing will grow your communication skills. The worst thing you can do is to avoid situations that make you uncomfortable because of the communication aspect. Role play with each other, read your word tracks, and practice with three customers each day. You'll discover you'll get more and more comfortable up until you don't even notice the awkwardness anymore.

- Hold regular shop meetings between service writers and technicians designed to encourage communication.

- Utilize Customer Problem Analysis Sheets to help collect pertinent customer concern information.

- Encourage technicians to bring service writers into the shop to explain the problem and associated repair.

- Challenging customers need to be listened to and have empathy expressed.

- Offer solutions to upset customers – not excuses or reasons something happened.

Chapter 4: Service Writers

> ## In This Chapter
>
> - **Finding good service writers.**
> - **Service writer skill set**
> - **Service writer pay plans**

Service writers are, to me, the most critical link in any service department. They are the "face" of the business, interact constantly with customers, technicians, and management, and have to be able to sell needed maintenance and repairs. Often times they are asked to understand technical problems and diagnostic procedures that they haven't been trained for, must deal patiently with upset customers, and often have to make sure technicians earn a decent paycheck (depending on the repair shop's pay system).

The service writer role is one of management, communication, and sales. A good service writer understands people, is patient, and has good organizational and communication skills. A good service writer can really grow your business, and a bad one can cause irreparable harm. You probably already know how difficult it is to find a quality service writer!

Finding a Service Writer

So where do you go to find a service writer? What qualities should you look for in a service writer? Who makes a good service writer?

Something to Consider

Some of the best service writers can be found in sales positions in and out of the automotive industry.

Of the best service writers I've known in my career, one was a former school teacher, one an HR professional with a background in psychology, and one a former automotive dealership salesperson. What did each of these folks have in common? They each had a way with people. First and foremost, they understood people and knew how to really make a connection with people.

In any business, customer relationships can make or break the business. Especially in a business where the customer is already anxious when they walk through the door, it is imperative that you put people in place who understand the customers they will be dealing with.

Where should you go looking when you need to hire a new service writer? You can advertise in all the usual places: newspapers, online employment websites, and local publications. This will of course attract all sorts of responses.

Key Point

Spread the word that you are hiring through your daily and weekly contacts with parts delivery drivers and tool truck representatives.

As with many things in business, often your best solution is to rely on your network. Mention to your employees that you are looking for someone (if they don't already know). Often times someone knows a person with whom they worked in the past, and will get word to them of an opportunity. Word of mouth sometimes generates the best leads. Although it occasionally can backfire on you, this can be a great way to build a strong team that works well together.

Key Point

For Service Advisor Training visit: **www.shop-pros.com.**

Spreading the word among your daily industry contacts such as tool dealers, parts representatives, and other association members can yield you good candidates. You always want to be careful not to gain the reputation as the business who steals employees from others, but letting a parts driver know you're looking to fill a position can be a gentle way of getting word to others in town.

```
Something to Consider

Just because a person is a low performer at one posi-
tion, doesn't mean that they won't be a high performer
in a different position.
```

You might also speak with your local vocational school to see if they have any students about to graduate who fit your criteria. I'm a big proponent of building relationships with your local technical education school whether it be a secondary (high school), or post-secondary (college) program. The more you support the local school by sitting on an advisory committee, accepting students looking for an internship, or serving in some other capacity, the more likely you are to be given a good lead by an instructor.

```
Customer Satisfaction Point

If you are in a position to employ more than one service
writer be sure to match your writers to your customer
base. Diversity can help your business to grow.
```

Don't be afraid to contact other business owners that you know who employ salespeople. There may be someone looking to move along an underperformer who will jump at the chance to pass the word along. I've seen cases where this very thing happened. The business owner needed to move a salesperson along to fill the spot with someone more productive but didn't have enough reason to let the individual go out right.

When the owner approached the salesperson with another job opportunity that offered more consistent pay, the salesperson interviewed and got the job. The service writer position fit the salesperson far better because of the more consistent paycheck and lesser amount of selling pressure. The salesperson went on to excel at being a service writer and his former boss got to fill his spot with a better performer. It was a win, win, win, situation! A secondary lesson from this story is that just because someone isn't very good at one job, doesn't mean that they won't be excellent at another.

As in all businesses and organizations, diversity will benefit your business. It doesn't matter whether the service writer is a man or a woman, or what race the individual is. More than anything they must be able to empathize and communicate with people. If I had my choice I'd always have one male service writer and one female service writer. We each have a type of person who we are comfortable dealing with and with whom we are confident in building a trust relationship.

> **Key Point**
>
> Establish a strong relationship with your area secondary or post-secondary vocational programs. Doing so can help you "grow" some great employees.

Having both a male and a female service writer can help build lasting relationships with more of your customers, more quickly.

Consider any specific language challenges you experience in your market. I've known repair shops who hired a service writer who spoke a specific language because the neighborhood in which they were situated was primarily populated with people of Asian descent. In this situation, although the customers were from many different Asian speaking countries, the owner discovered that there was a dialect of the language that they could all understand. He then set out to find a service writer who could speak that specific dialect. His business almost doubled the first year after hiring the new service writer!

Above all, you need your customers to feel comfortable dealing with your service writer(s). It's easier to teach a service writer what they need to know about the automotive business than it is to teach them how to connect with people.

Key Point

It's easier to teach someone about the automotive business than it is to teach them to deal well with people. Look for service writers who are good with people first.

Look for individuals who come from backgrounds where they had to interact with many different people, and those who enjoy dealing with different people every day. When hiring for a service writer position you're looking for people persons foremost.

Service Writer Pay Plans

Like many things in our industry, pay plans can be as simple, or as complicated as you want them to be. Some owners like to pay their people just to show up and be present in the workplace all day. Other shop owners want to incentivize certain behaviors and so may pay on a commission or bonus basis.

No matter what pay plan you choose to implement, it should serve a specific purpose. Pay plans aren't just compensation for doing a specific job, but they are tools to create and grow your business. Pay plans engage your employees and your business.

Pay plans can be tricky and are seldom liked by everyone. Pay plans should be seen as tools. Tools to both attract and retain quality employees, and tools to grow the business.

Key Point

Use pay plans as tools to improve specific aspects of your business. They should both attract, and retain quality employees.

There is always a method to offering a particular pay plan, and like anything else in business, one group's pay plan does not function in isolation. When structuring pay plans you will need to keep in mind what your goal for the pay plan is, and how one group's pay plan may affect another group's pay plan (i.e. if you pay your service writers a straight hourly wage, but your technicians are being paid flat rate, is there incentive for the service writers to sell the work the technicians are recommending?).

The idea behind service writer pay plans is to create a situation where the individual is not only paid for the work that they do, but they are also financially encouraged to grow your business. Many service writer pay plans are commission based in some manner. Carefully constructed, commission based pay plans, can be used to focus business growth in very specific areas, or to encourage specific behavior.

As a business owner whose business relies on high levels of customer satisfaction and the associated customer retention, you want to make sure that you are incentivizing the right behaviors. Creating a pay plan that incentivizes the wrong behavior can have a harmful effect on your business and negate the original intent of the pay plan. You need to balance the requirement to sell labor and parts with an acceptable level of customer satisfaction.

However you structure the pay plan, you want to be sure that you are basing the incentive on something that the service writer can control. For instance if you are going to pay your writer a base salary plus a dollar figure for every tire he or she sells, but you have trouble keeping tires in inventory because of a world-wide shortage of rubber, you've created a situation where the writer can't possibly improve tire sales for

---

Key Point

Make sure to base any pay plan incentives on variables that can be controlled. Basing pay on variables that are out of the control of the service writer will only result in an unhappy employee.

---

you or their own paycheck, through no fault of their own. This will only result in a frustrated and unhappy employee, and the possibility of high turnover.

You will also want to make sure that you base any incentive pay on something that you can measure. If you want to drive customer satisfaction increases but have no way of gauging customer satisfaction with some sort of concrete number then you've set yourself up for an argument with your service writer each week! In this case it may be better to identify some behavior that you feel will improve customer satisfaction.

Choose a behavior that you can objectively measure. For instance, say we want to increase customer satisfaction and we've somehow identified (even anecdotally) that our customers aren't as happy as they could be because of multiple repair attempts for the same problem. In other words, our fixed-right-first-time isn't what it should be. How can we measure whether we've increased customer satisfaction based on this metric?

> ### Customer Satisfaction Point
>
> Take care to incentivize the right behaviors. Monitor your pay plans to ensure they haven't had an unexpected negative effect in another area.

An easy, and simple, way might be to monitor the number of "comebacks". Comebacks could be defined as customers that returned to your shop for the same complaint within a certain time period. This can generally be monitored through most electronic management systems used in the repair shop industry, or if you're not using an electronic system, it is usually known throughout your shop which customer was just in for what complaint. Pointing this out to the service writer won't usually create much of an argument.

Customer Satisfaction Point

Whether you incentivize a lower number of comebacks, or not, it's always a good idea to monitor how many comebacks each technician is responsible for.

Since we are trying to incentivize fewer "comebacks" we should think about what we ultimately want to accomplish. What behavior modification do we want to make? Maybe it is a case where communication between the technician and service writer needs to improve. Or maybe we need to get the service writer to improve the information collected from the customer. No matter what we've identified as the root cause of too many comebacks, we need to give the service writer the education and tools to fix it, and then incentivize them to do so.

In our previous example we might pay the service writer a base salary and then a bonus on top of that for every week the comeback number stays below whatever number we've deemed acceptable (it might even be zero comebacks). Now you might be thinking "but the technician has more to do with comebacks than the writer does" and in some cases, you wouldn't be wrong. You may be able to improve overall technician performance through the service writer however.

We're still paying the service writer on a quantifiable aspect of customer satisfaction.

Paying a service writer to reduce the number of comebacks might not only increase their attention on collecting customer concern information, but may also encourage them to improve communication with the technicians. It may even encourage them to help quality control the vehicle before returning it to the customer. So even though the technician has the ultimate responsibility for the repair, we've encouraged the service writer to take a more active role in ensuring a proper repair.

Here are some other examples of pay plans:

- Base Salary + % of labor sales + Customer Satisfaction Bonus = Total Weekly Pay (incentivizes up-selling repairs and maintenance as well as customer satisfaction).

- Base Salary + % of labor sales + $1 for every tire sold = Total Weekly Pay (incentivizes up-selling repairs and maintenance as well as tire sales for the week).

- % labor sales + Customer Satisfaction Bonus + $10 for every cooling system service sold = Total Weekly Pay (incentivizes up-selling repairs and maintenance, customer satisfaction, and a seasonal service that was recently marketed).

- Base salary + $1 an hour increase for every technician flat rate hour sold over 40, $2 an hour over 50 hours, $3 an hour over 60 hours, etc. = Total Weekly Pay (incentivizes up-selling repairs and maintenance as well as helps to encourage shop productivity).

Service writer pay plans can be manipulated in many ways, to incentivize many different things. There will be times when you'll want to incentivize the selling of certain products or services, promote shop efficiency, increase customer satisfaction, or just plain increase shop productivity. It could be as simple as needing to change certain behaviors your service writers have become accustomed to.

Keep in mind that you don't want your service writers struggling to make a paycheck; you want them struggling to reach a goal and make a bonus. There is a big difference. The right pay plan will attract and retain good employees. The wrong pay plan may cost you good employees and worse yet, cost you customers. Always make sure you are incentivizing the right behaviors.

Don't be afraid to experiment, or to discover that your plan didn't work! Sometimes we think the plan will incentivize the right thing only to discover it created an unexpected behavior or negative result! Just be sure to give the pay plan enough time to adequately show whether the numbers, or behavior, change before trying something new.

Something to Consider

Don't be afraid to experiment and fail. Be sure to give any new pay plan time to work. Performance is sure to drop before the changes take hold and you realize the gains you expected. Be patient!

Study after study has shown that when any change is implemented, there is almost always an immediate drop in production, or results, before the new way of doing things takes hold and eventually creates increases over pre-change results or productivity. Give it an appropriate amount of time to work!

No matter what you want to incentivize you must always remember:

- Whatever metric you want to pay for must be *objective* and *measurable*.
- The service writer must be able to *control* the conditions that will result in accomplishing your goal.
- Don't incentivize something that will have a negative effect on another part of your business.
- The service writer must always be able to make a base amount of pay commensurate with the cost of living in your area.
- Give it *time* to work!

On-Boarding Employees

As important as finding the right employees, and connecting them to a great pay plan is, even more important might be having a formal on-boarding process. If you were to research statistics around on-boarding, you'd find that employees who a put through a formal program stay with the employer, on average, four years longer than those who have not completed a formal program. New-hire employees are also more than sixty percent more productive during the first sixty days. The statistics go on from there, but every statistic shows that you really do need to have a formal on-boarding program.

Employee onboarding may sound like a luxury—after all, can't your other employees help new hires get the hang of things? How hard is writing a repair order when they already know how to do it on a different system? —but the truth is, good onboarding is an essential part of communicating expectations and culture, as well as a necessary part of limiting turnover. There are statistics that suggest employees who participate in an onboarding process remain on the job years longer than those who do not participate in an onboarding process. Want to limit turnover? Have an onboarding process!

Good onboarding is all about setting the right tone for your new hires.

If you can get employees off to the right start, they are far more likely to find job satisfaction and success—and you are far less likely to be disappointed with their work. The "right start" may look different in each organization, and may be somewhat subjective, but having a formal plan will ensure that, whatever a "right start" means in your organization, you'll accomplish it. On-boarding is like service writer training, but different. They'll still learn how to write a repair order in your system, deliver exceptional customer service the way you want it done, learn your processes, and build relationships with your existing employees. They will also become a part of your organizational culture, not feel like they are an outsider, and have low enough anxiety that they'll be able to learn and grow into their role.

The First Thirty Days Are Everything

The first thirty days are everything when it comes to setting the tone and saving yourself later pain, and good hiring makes onboarding easier—yet another reason to always be hiring. Unlike a training class, on-boarding takes a longer period of time. Just like a service writer training class, onboarding is not a "learn it and just do it" kind of venture. Onboarding teaches service advisors how the entire system works, makes them feel at home and welcome, and allows them to ask questions, improve performance, and get their feet on the ground for a solid foundation.

Of course, new hires with some level of experience in a shop like yours can make starting their work routine easier—but you still have to communicate exactly what your expectations are and how accountability in your shop works, and that's where onboarding comes in. New hires come with the potential to bring new habits to the organization – good habits, and some not-so-good habits. Likewise, the danger to culture development within your organization is the person that takes the new hire under his or her wing and says "I know the boss says to do it like this, but let me show you how we really do it here". Institutional knowledge, whether related to customer service, writing repair orders, answering the phone, or any other aspect of the service writer job, is both powerful in developing an organization, and a barrier to change. A well thought out and executed on-boarding process will help to both bring the new hire up to speed comfortably and quickly, as well as ensure the overall culture continues to grow and mature.

Have A Plan, Goals, And Priorities

Before you onboard a new service writer, you need a plan for what that onboarding will ideally look like. Not only does a plan help keep you organized when you are onboarding the new hire, but it helps the organization around you know what to expect, too. The more you can define this, the better; if the new hire also knows what to expect in their onboarding process, all the better.

Creating an onboarding process will take time, energy, and effort. That's what you're here for! Again, it's not just a training program for a new service writer. They already know how to treat customers well, but they need to understand what your expectations are, what tools they have available at your auto shop service counter, and how your system makes it easy to write repair orders and estimates.

I've split the development of the program into three days so that nobody feels overwhelmed and so that you'll have time to digest the idea of the program, developing the plan, and managing the plan. Developing, and executing the onboarding plan will be the next major business development that you will be able to pass along to your manager so that he or she understands the expectation and has possibly already experienced the result.

Developing Your Plan

Your onboarding plan will want to lay out the priorities, goals and milestones for the new employee at 30, 60, and 90 day intervals. Every organization, and business book for that matter, suggests a different routine for onboarding depending on the established organizational culture. None of them are wrong. The one thing they all agree on however is that onboarding should not be rushed.

DO NOT rush employee onboarding. Doing so will limit your organizational growth.

Before you build out your full ninety-day plan, you will develop an initial plan that will cover:

- Before The Employee Begins
- The First Day
- The Second Day
- The First Week
- The Second Week

In general, your goal for onboarding an employee is not just to allow them to get up to speed as fast as possible and become a productive employee, but rather to allow the employee a chance to learn, observe, understand, get comfortable, and know the overall organization. **Never underestimate the value of an employee knowing the aspects of the organization that are not directly related to their job.** An observational understanding of how every aspect of your business works in concert helps new service writers see the larger role their part plays, and it's important you don't rush that, lest you risk not developing that understanding, which is an important part of developing your organizational culture. This is more than just a training program – it is the development of a thorough understanding of your customer service expectations, repair order expectations, and other process expectations.

Watching everyone involved—technicians, receptionists, service, etc.—helps new hires gain a better understanding of how each piece works in your organizational system, regardless of what their responsibilities may be.

Very few people operate well under pressure – whether you think they should be able to or not, and they certainly don't learn well under pressure. Removing the stress from the first 30 days, while intentionally guiding a new employee through development will create the employee you thought you'd hired.

Not only does setting those priorities and goals ahead of time help hold new employees accountable, but they help hold you and your team accountable, too. If a new hire isn't meeting those milestone goals, everyone involved can examine why not—is it a problem with the new hire's work, or have they simply not been given the skills or tools they need to reach those goals?

Your onboarding plan should have priorities, goals, and milestones, ideally at 30, 60, and 90 days.

On-Boarding Considerations

When an employee begins their employment, on day one, be sure to act like they are here to stay. There is a very different message sent when an employee shows up and isn't provided logins, passwords, business cards, uniforms, etc. If you believe you've hired the right person, act like you hired the right person! By providing uniforms and business cards on the first day, an employee already feels like part of the team. If they don't work out, yes, you're out a bit of money, but not anything that will break your organization. By not providing those things on the first day, they still feel like an outsider. This is just as important for the existing personnel to see. I've watched organizations that were brutal to new hires in that they had an "us against them" mentality until the new employee proved themselves. An organization like this is destined for employee turnover and slow growth.

Make the first day memorable and relaxed. Use this day to complete paperwork, discuss lunch and break polices, do some observations, check on logins and passwords, create a bio for the website, and maybe do a lunch 'n learn with all the employees to reintroduce everyone. I understand that there's a tendency to want someone new to experience the true nature of the organization on the first day, but remember that if you operate a busy shop, you might do more damage than good by fully immersing someone in the chaos on the first day. This is true even with someone who comes to the job with experience.

The first week should be kept simple and focused on the key components of your business that an service writer really needs to know, understand, and execute. I understand that everything is important in your eyes, yet you didn't learn it all at once either! Take some time to think about which tasks, processes or procedures are foundational to the success of your organization. This is also a great time to consider where you want to set a new tone and which processes are not being done consistently enough by existing service writers. You have a chance to start someone off on a different foot, while at the same time affecting the current culture in a positive way. Some even decide existing employees should not attend any more training until they do through a similar on-boarding process. Take the time to get it right and you'll reap the reward of well-written repair orders, exceptional customer service, the best service writers in town, and a great reputation for years to come. I believe so strongly in the importance of on-boarding that each of our coaching programs is given a formal on-boarding plan for their repair shops.

In Conclusion

Service writers are one of your most critical assets. Choosing the right service writer will be a significant key to growing and optimizing your repair shop. When looking for service writers look for someone who is a people person, has strong organizational skills, and who may come from a sales background.

Give your service writers the tools that they need to do their job effectively and efficiently and you will see your business grow. Challenge your service writers to grow and improve your business by modifying their pay plans. Encourage communication between service writers and your technicians, and constantly review your customer satisfaction practices. Helping your service writers to understand the importance of customer satisfaction by providing them the tools they need to initiate your customer satisfaction programs will grow your business to levels not seen before.

- **Look for service writers in industries other than automotive repair.**
- **Service writers need strong people skills more than an automotive background.**
- **Ask your network (parts delivery people, tool truck representatives, trade organizations, etc.) if they know anyone interested in becoming a service writer.**
- **Don't neglect individuals working in sales positions outside the automotive industry.**
- **When creating incentivized pay plans make sure:**
    - Whatever metric you want to pay for is *objective* and *measurable*.
    - The service writer is able to *control* the conditions that will accomplish the goal.
    - You don't incentivize something that will have a negative effect on another part of your business.
    - You give it *time* to work.

Chapter 5: Technicians

In This Chapter

- **Technician skill set.**
- **Finding technicians.**
- **Technician pay plans.**

Technicians are extremely important to your business, for reasons different than service writers are important. As with service writers, finding good technicians can be a significant challenge to an auto repair shop. Technicians must possess mechanical, diagnostic, and communication skills. They must have solid work practices, take pride in their work, and be able to continually learn.

The really good technicians continually seek out training material and always strive to learn new technologies. An important thing to remember about technicians is that, in general, they function well in an environment where they are given the tools to do their job, the time and space to do their job, and are incentivized to be productive.

Technician Skill Set

In an ideal world we all have an idea of what we want our technicians to be like. If I were to design the ideal technician here are some of the things I would want:

- Is willing to learn.
- Takes pride in their work quality.
- Has some sort of education whether its college or vocational school.
- Is comfortable with and around computers.
- Has some automotive background.
- Presents well.
- Posses some mentoring ability.

Of course this would be in an ideal world. In the real world, however, we find technicians who are quirky, don't present well, rush through their work, don't want to admit when they're wrong, are not comfortable with computers, and are not well-educated. So where do we find technicians that possess some of our ideal world characteristics, who we can train to become the technicians that will help our business grow?

Finding Technicians

By far the best way I know of finding technicians is to grow your own. By that I mean find a young individual who wants to work in the automotive industry as a mechanic or technician, and train them to become that ideal technician. This sounds like a major undertaking, but it is surprisingly easy to do. Granted it takes time and perseverance, but can pay tremendous dividends.

The first step in growing your own technician is to identify a young person you know who is interested in automobile repair, who shows promise, and then begin a mentoring process. Again, this is an area where you can partner with local vocational centers to find individuals to develop as technicians. A vocational school or community college can not only help you find an individual, but they can help you develop a quality mentoring program at your shop.

Key Point

Quality technicians can be tough to find. "Growing your own" is by far the best way to acquire them. Establish relationships with nearby technical schools and learn to work with students. It will pay dividends to you in the long term.

There are certainly challenges to working with vocational students and growing them into the technicians, but the rewards can be tremendous. Their success is not always immediate, and sometimes it takes time and patience to grow them into the technician you desire. I would encourage anyone reading this book to visit the local vocational automotive instructor and talk to them about what sort of partnership you might develop with their program.

Usually working with vocational programs involves regular turnover of students who you are working with. This can be a challenge, but with the proper mentor and attention to forming a relationship with your repair shop, you may find the student comes back to you after high school or college graduation. Many repair shops have successfully grown co-op students or interns into valuable long-term employees.

The second step to growing your own technicians is having somebody in the shop, whether it's yourself or another technician, who can properly mentor the future technician. This is why, when hiring technicians, I am always looking for someone who has previously worked with students or young people in some capacity, not necessarily just in an automotive learning capacity. Vocational co-op students will not have all of the knowledge, skills, or motivation that will eventually be required. A good mentor knows how to motivate a student, develop a student's pride in their work, and can effectively challenge a co-op student to learn and grow.

Something to Consider

Mentoring co-op students can be challenging. Seek help, through your school partnerships, to learn how to mentor students.

As with most any employee, the key to proper development of a vocational school student, and really any technician, is to have a plan. Work with the local vocational instructor to develop a plan for the co-op student, and make sure their mentor works with the student to accomplish that plan.

This means regular reviews of the plan, what they've learned, what they want to learn, and how their performance has improved. Be encouraging, be honest, and persuade the student to ask questions. Managing a co-op student is really not unlike managing any other employee. They may need a little more encouragement and positive reinforcement to become a valuable technician for your repair shop, but they can become some of your most valuable human assets.

Key Point

Have a plan to work with co-op students. Doing so will help with the buy-in of the student, mentor, and other technicians. Review the plan weekly.

One other note for working with co-op students is to give them challenging work once in a while. At the very least, let them team with another technician on a challenging problem. Many of us came into the business changing oil, rotating tires, and sweeping the floor, but to a student who is trying to decide what they want to do after they leave school this isn't much incentive to stay in the business. The employee market has changed dramatically over the last 30 years. Let them know that everyone should pull their own weight. Set the expectation that they will be asked to change oil, rotate tires, and clean the shop a majority of time, but that you will also provide them the opportunity to do the more "exciting" stuff. Try to strike a balance between the student learning the business, learning to repair cars, and utilizing them as "an extra body" or "go-fer".

If you don't currently have a process in place to grow your own technicians, you are left with advertising or word-of-mouth to find a technician. Once again, you can advertise in all the usual places: newspapers, automotive publications, local job boards, internet job boards, etc. Don't forget to check with your tool representatives, parts representatives, and other business contacts for individuals who may be looking to change jobs, or become technicians. These business people see a lot of repair shops in their travels and usually have a pretty good idea of who is available, or who might become available, in the area.

Key Point

Have a written interview plan. Write your questions down before you go into the interview. You're looking for someone who is a learner and who will potentially make a great employee – not someone who just looks good on paper.

The challenge you face once you get people to respond to your advertisement or inquiries is to interview the individual so you can identify a potential new technician that will help you grow your business. Many managers are not comfortable interviewing people. If you have a track record of not being able to choose the appropriate individual, or if you are one of those who are not comfortable interviewing others, then it is a good idea to have a formal written plan for the interview process. Even if you are comfortable interviewing people, this will help you feel more confident in your interviewing skills and make it less likely that you forget to ask an important question. Don't be afraid to interview an individual more than once. I generally recommend a four step interview process.

Suggested Four-Step Interview Process

1. Telephone Interview
2. In-person, off-site interview (lunch)
3. In-person, on-site interview
4. Job offer made to both candidate and spouse

So how do you interview an individual to give yourself the best chance of finding a quality technician? As with most anything, interviewing is not perfect. There will be times when you think you've identified someone who fits all the requirements of a good technician only to find out a few weeks later that you hired the wrong person.

What should you ask during the interview? What should you look for during the interview? Following are a few things I look for when interviewing potential technicians (not necessarily in order). None of these, by itself, is a deal breaker:

- Does the technician have current ASE certification? Why or why not?
- How does the technician feel about talking to customers?
- How did the applicant come to be a technician or mechanic (background)?
- Why does the technician want to work for an independent repair shop versus a dealership?

- What does the technician like about the auto repair industry, and what don't they like about the auto repair industry?
- What service information databases is the technician familiar with?
- What scan tool(s) is the technician comfortable using?
- What are the technician's views on technical training?
- Have they ever worked with high school or college co-op students?

The above questions are only a few things you might ask during the interview. The purpose of these questions is to determine the technician' s motivation for being in the business, whether they might be a good fit for developing relationships with customers, and to judge their motivation for continuing education.

The best that you can do is to develop an interview and hiring process that gives you a good indication of whether a certain individual fits your requirements. The hiring process should include an interview, a background check, a drug test, and a probation period.

Remember that during the interview process you are not just trying to find someone who has the technical ability to fix cars, or diagnose problems, but someone who can truly help your business grow. You're looking for someone who can help your business develop relationships with your customers, someone who can work with your service writer efficiently, and someone who ultimately will treat your business as if it were their own.

Technician Pay Plans

Technicians always want to know how they're going to get paid. Just like with service writers, there is more than one way to pay the technician for performing their duties. Technician duties may vary from shop to shop. Duties may also vary depending on an individual's previous experience or the role you need to fill within the shop. Common ways for independent repair shops to pay their technicians is either with an hourly wage or by using a flat rate pay system. You might also consider combining the two to capitalize on the best of both systems and help eliminate some of the negatives found in each system.

Hourly Wage

Paying a technician an hourly wage means you pay them to be at the shop. This means the technician is being paid from the time they show up for work in the morning, until the time they punch out when they leave for home at the end of the day, no matter how productive they may be. Most repair shops give technicians who are on an hourly wage pay system regular breaks during the day as well as a lunch break. The length of the breaks and lunch may vary from shop to shop.

Key Point

Hourly wage pay plans can be great in certain shops where the technicians are needed to do jobs other than just work on vehicles.

The challenge with this type of pay system is that there is no incentive for technicians to perform their work quickly, or to increase their efficiency or productivity. Many technicians who know they are not efficient in their work practices, or who choose not to work quickly, prefer this pay system. Some technicians prefer hourly pay systems because they don't feel any pressure to be productive. Some days, when they're feeling up to it, they'll get a ton of work done. On days they don't feel like being so productive, they can relax and it doesn't affect how much money they'll make.

A positive aspect to paying a technician an hourly wage is that the technician is not losing money during diagnosis of difficult problems, when speaking with customers, or performing duties other than vehicle repair. If you are a small independent repair shop and have a need for your technicians to do more than just repair and diagnose vehicles you may want to consider an hourly wage pay system to start with.

Although straight time, or hourly pay systems, have their positives, they can keep your business from growing.

Key Point

The down-side to hourly pay plans is that they don't create much incentive for technicians to help grow revenues.

Flat Rate

Another frequently used a system in the automotive industry, possibly the most commonly used, is the flat rate pay scale. This is where each technician gets paid to perform an operation based upon a documented time for completion of that operation. This system encourages productivity because the technician gets paid a specific time for an operation whether they complete the operation in less time or more time. If the technician can "beat flat rate" he or she can make more money in a workday than they would if being paid an hourly wage.

Key Point

Flat-rate pay systems are terrific productivity drivers. Quality control systems should be put in place to ensure high levels of customer satisfaction however.

The benefit of the flat rate pay system is in increased productivity. Technicians have the ability to be paid for more hours than they are physically at work. For instance, if a technician completes a number of jobs, or service operations, in a single day that add up to 12.5 hours of work, he or she gets paid that number of hours times a flat rate hourly wage. This means that the technician physically worked eight hours but will be paid 12.5 hours. In this manner technicians are encouraged to become highly productive during the time which they are at work. If they are not working, they are not getting paid. The flat rate hourly wage is generally slightly less than a straight time hourly wage, so in some instances technicians get paid the same overall amount as they would if they worked hourly; however, the shop gets the benefit of increased productivity.

The negative aspect of flat rate pay systems is that some technicians are encouraged to shortcut the job. Rushing through a job in order to "beat flat rate" can be bad for business, or worse for business, than paying a technician to not be productive. With some technicians, flat rate pay systems put undue pressure on them to perform.

Another negative flat rate pay systems can create is that technicians often don't get paid for diagnosis of problems. This can create a situation where technicians are more likely to "throw parts" at a repair rather than properly diagnosing the repair. They would rather guess at a solution and move onto the better paying service or maintenance job than spend time diagnosing a problem that they may not get paid for. There are ways to work around some of the negatives of flat-rate pay systems while maintaining the positive aspects of this system.

To counter technicians rushing through jobs to "beat flat rate" certain quality control checks can be put in place. Implementing quality control processes utilizing other technicians or service writers can help ensure quality flat rate work is done. However, this requires someone in the shop who has the ability and authority to quality control the work.

Something to Consider

Many technicians prefer to work flat rate because of the earning potential. If a technician isn't comfortable working flat rate, then you may have to find a more suitable position for them.

If you don't have someone who has the time, authority, or qualifications to quality control every vehicle leaving the shop, then you may want to consider combining flat rate and hourly pay systems as laid out in the next section. This can provide the productivity benefits of flat rate, with the quality benefits of hourly pay systems. To avoid the "shopping cart diagnostic approach" created by flat rate pay systems, shop owners and service managers may choose to pay technicians "straight time" for diagnostic work. This means the technician will be paid a straight hourly wage for the amount of time it takes he or she to diagnose the problem. The technician then gets paid a flat rate time to remove and replace the associated part or parts, or repair the problem. This is a common workaround for this particular negative aspect of flat-rate pay systems that both technicians and repair shops are comfortable with. The challenge is still there of keeping a technician from poorly executing a diagnosis so that they can move on to a better paying service job. For most technicians, knowing that they are getting paid something for diagnosis is enough for them to dedicate some time to more accurately diagnosing the problem though.

As for technicians who feel that flat-rate pay systems put too much pressure on them, it might be suggested that these technicians are better suited for another position within your shop. Technicians who are generally proficient within their profession prefer to work flat-rate because of the amount of money that they can make. If a technician is adamantly against working flat rate, this might be a red flag to the owner or manager that this individual may not be very productive. If they seem to be well qualified, with a significant amount of experience, and just don't think that they can keep up with flat rate production demands, then you can often find a different position, or pay plan for them that will make everyone comfortable.

Many repair shops prefer flat-rate because it can drive productivity and ultimately increase labor sales for the repair shop.

Combining Hourly Wage and Flat Rate Systems

Sometimes the solution to making technicians feel comfortable with their work environment and encouraging productivity is a combination of hourly and flat-rate systems. As discussed previously, hourly wage systems allow the technician to be paid for doing jobs, such as diagnosis, for which there is not necessarily a "book time". Flat-rate systems drive productivity, but may not pay technicians for diagnosis. Combining an hourly wage pay plan with some sort of production bonus plan can capture the best of both pay systems.

One such system might pay a technician a base pay rate, whether it be an hourly wage, or a salary, and add to that a bonus based on the total flat-rate hours a technician turns in a week. For instance, a technician is paid $10 an hour for every hour they are present at work (hourly rate). During the work week they are required to take a time punch for every operation that they perform on a vehicle and record the associated flat rate time (book time) for that job. At the end of the week the flat-rate hours are added and the technician is paid a bonus hourly wage for those hours over 40 for which he turned flat-rate.

Generally in this type of system the technicians are paid a slightly lower hourly wage. The hourly wage is set so that the technician makes the salary equivalent of a 30 to 35 hour workweek, but can easily make the equivalent of a 45 to 50

Key Point

Combining an hourly pay plan system with a production bonus can capitalize on the best of hourly and flat-rate pay systems.

---

hour workweek by turning more than 40 flat rate hours. This accomplishes two things. Firstly, the technician receives a steady paycheck every week no matter how many flat-rate hours they turn. Secondly, this pay system encourages productivity by allowing the technician to make additional money for turning out more work. To me, and for many technicians, it's a best of both worlds scenario. It doesn't always eliminate the "I'm not being paid for diagnosis" argument, but at the very least you can now point out that they are being paid for that coffee break they just took!

Key Point

When creating a combined pay system for your repair shop, the salary portion of the plan is generally set so that the technicians will make around 30 hours worth of straight time pay for the week.

As with service writer pay plans there are many ways of creating technician pay plans by combining both salary, and hourly wages plans, with bonus incentives. Often times repair shops will want to incentivize certain aspects of the business. Technician pay plans can be used just like service writer pay plans to improve customer satisfaction, efficiency, productivity, and parts sales. Bonuses can be paid technicians for up-selling seasonal services, wiper blades, tires, etc.. When managing a plan the shop owner or service manager must always balance customer satisfaction, employee satisfaction, and business goals.

Always Remember

- Growing your own technicians is by far the best way of acquiring quality technicians.
- Create and nurture relationships with local vocational and community college automotive programs.
- Combine hourly and flat-rate pay plans to capitalize on the positive aspects of both, and help eliminate some of the negative aspects.
- Use technician pay plans to incentivize shop productivity, parts sales, increased customer satisfaction.

Chapter 6: Tools for Technicians

> **In This Chapter**
>
> - Alignment equipment.
> - Scan tools.
> - Technical training.
> - Other shop equipment.

As with any employee, technicians must be provided the tools they need to perform their job properly. Having the right tools available ensures proper diagnosis and repair, and ultimately provides for customer satisfaction. Some tools technicians are expected to provide, while others the shop is expected to provide. Tools can increase productivity, accuracy, and efficiency, and at the same time they can be a source of constant aggravation.

Shop Equipment

All technicians hired are to have their own hand tools. These include common tools like wrenches, pliers, screwdrivers, and others, as well as diagnostic tools such as a digital volt ohm meter (DVOM), fuel pressure gauge, vacuum gauge, and other "small" diagnostic devices. Other tools designated as "shop equipment" are to be provided by the place of employment. These tools are used by all technicians in the repair shop.

Equipment such as alignment machines, tire mounting and balancing equipment, hydraulic presses, puller kits, air conditioning equipment, and scan tool diagnostic equipment are generally expected to be provided by the repair shop. This equipment represents a significant initial capital investment and technicians should be held accountable for the proper operation, safety, and use of this equipment. This is an area that often receives little attention, but results in expensive repair and replacement costs to virtually every repair shop.

Key Point

Technicians need to be properly trained on all shop equipment. They need to be held accountable for the proper operation, use, and safety of the equipment commonly used in the shop.

Each new technician hired by the repair shop should be properly trained on the use, operation, and safety aspects of all shop equipment. "Trust but verify" should be a common practice when hiring new technicians and exposing them to your particular brand of shop equipment. Most technicians like to think that they know how to operate all the equipment found in a shop, or at the very least, like to think that they can "figure it out". Providing formal training to new hires can reduce the learning time, eliminate potentially costly mistakes, and ensure the safety of both your technicians, and your shop equipment. Never assume new hires know how to use the equipment found in your shop. Always provide them with adequate training!

Sources of training may include other technicians, yourself, or an outside trainer. If you don't have anyone in the shop with whom you feel comfortable tasking the training of new hires, then seek outside help. Most equipment suppliers have someone who can provide your technicians with training on the equipment they sell. For more complete training, or training on a wider range of equipment, contact a company specializing in automotive technical training.

Key Point

Sources of training for the proper use of shop equipment can be a qualified technician in your shop, an outside professional trainer, or an equipment representative.

I strongly encourage repair shops to keep equipment in good repair, perform regular maintenance, and consistently update all of their shop equipment. By doing so you not only improve customer satisfaction by increasing "fixed-right-first-time," but you will also send a message to your technicians that you care about your customers and the job your technicians do for your customers. Poorly maintained shop equipment sends the message to the technicians that the shop doesn't care about the technicians or the quality of the work performed for the customer. Inadequately maintained equipment also costs the shop owner money in down time and replacement costs.

Alignment Equipment

Alignment machines and the associated lift, while expensive, generally have a rapid return on investment. Alignment measuring equipment, although often packaged with a lift, can be purchased separately from the actual lift. You don't have to buy the alignment equipment manufacturer's lift just because it matches the measuring equipment. A separate, self-leveling, four-post or scissor lift from another manufacturer can be utilized.

The software for the alignment machine needs to be kept up-to-date so that the proper specifications for vehicle alignment are available to the technician. Some shops choose to update their alignment machine every other year rather than every year. This may be an acceptable practice based upon the demographic of your customer base. If your shop does not generally service brand-new vehicles then you may not have any need for the latest and greatest alignment specifications. However, if you are servicing brand-new vehicles and or do a lot of collision repair work, you will want to update your alignment software every six months.

The alignment lift, or alignment rack, must be well maintained for proper operation. The pneumatics, hydraulics, and all pivots should be properly maintained to avoid improperly performed alignments and technician safety issues. Set up a regular maintenance schedule for inspecting and servicing your alignment equipment. Early spring, or late summer are usually good times of year to perform this type of maintenance. You will want your equipment to be in top operating condition during the times of year when customers begin to think about tires!

During the winter months, especially in areas of the country where sand and salt is used on the roads, it is critical that the alignment rack be kept clean and free of debris. All moving and rotating parts should be cleaned weekly, if not daily. Doing so ensures longevity of the equipment, as well as high levels of customer satisfaction. Keeping the equipment clean and well maintained, will allow you to realize a superb return on investment!

Key Point

Purchase the best equipment you can afford and maintain it. Doing so will pay dividends to your bottom line.

Purchase the best equipment that you can afford. Today's alignment technology is essentially all the same, no matter the manufacturer. The differences between equipment come in the software package used to help the technician know when the vehicle is in alignment, or how to actually perform the mechanical processes used to align the vehicle. Other differences appear in after sale service and support. Let your technicians help you decide which equipment to purchase. Be sure to talk to them about what you're considering, and get their input. After all, they'll be the ones using it to make money for you! Talk to other shop owners about what equipment they use and what they like, and don't like, about it.

No matter what alignment equipment you choose to purchase, all of your technicians should be properly trained to utilize the equipment. Vehicle suspension service procedures change, requiring new knowledge to be acquired regularly. Proper training will avoid mistakes, ensure a quality repair, and increase customer satisfaction.

Air Conditioning Equipment

Many repairs within the engine compartment require the removal and recharging of vehicle air conditioning systems. You want to purchase quality air conditioning service equipment for the shop and have your technicians properly trained to use it. There is certain equipment that you will want to be sure to purchase while other equipment you may be able to wait on, but A/C equipment is a necessity.

Something to Consider

Alignment machine specifications should be updated yearly. If you are a low volume alignment shop then you may be able to get away with updating every other year.

A refrigerant identifier will help to avoid costly mistakes, and a possibly dangerous situation. The last thing that you want is to accidently recover a non-approved refrigerant with your recovery recycling machine as this creates an expensive disposal problem. Once you've recovered contaminated refrigerant you are legally responsible for any vehicle that the contaminated refrigerant is placed in, whether intentionally or accidentally. This can create a real nightmare for a repair shop.

Something to Consider

Make sure any technician who will be using the air conditioning equipment has their Section 609 Certification. They can take the test online for a nominal cost. **It is illegal for technicians to service air conditioning systems without this certification!**

In areas where there are a large number of vehicles entering the auction marketplace, it is common to find alternative refrigerants in AC systems. A repair shop needs to avoid contaminating existing stocks of R134a or R12 with each other or any alternative refrigerant.

In order to properly perform AC system service and repairs, a repair shop must have a refrigerant recovery/recycle machine. This is a device that will be used to recover refrigerant from a vehicle's AC system (after identifying what the refrigerant is). Once the repairs are completed, this machine will then be used to evacuate the AC system, and recharge the AC system safely and efficiently. Many of these machines can also store the refrigerant taken from the vehicle AC system and recycle it later.

At the very least you will need to purchase a machine that will recover and process R134a type refrigerant. The more expensive machines can be purchased with a built in refrigerant identifier. If you are in a position to spend the money, these are the machines I would consider. Your technicians are more likely to use the identifier if it's not a separate piece of equipment.

Be sure to purchase a good quality machine and keep it in proper operating condition. Filter changes, vacuum pump oil changes, and not using an extension cord to run the machine will help ensure a long, useful, and profitable life for your recovery/recycling machine.

Key Point

Assign the responsibility of informing management of broken or worn-out tools to a single technician in the shop.

Should you find an AC system that contains either a mix of refrigerants, or R12 refrigerant, you will need to utilize a separate machine to recover this contaminated refrigerant. There are specific machines available for the purpose of recovering contaminated, or mixed, refrigerant. These units are available at a lower cost than machines that are designed to handle a specific refrigerant.

There are new refrigerants currently being evaluated for mobile applications. It is likely that these new refrigerants will require a separate machine from your R134a machine. Keep this in mind when deciding what new equipment to purchase.

Presses and Pullers

Equipment such as hydraulic presses and puller kits tend to have a long lifespan with minimal maintenance. Of course this is assuming technicians utilize the equipment properly. Equipment in this category should be periodically inspected for wear, breakage, and missing pieces. This can be done by the shop owner, service manager, or delegated to a specific technician.

Key Point

By quickly replacing or repairing broken tools, shop management will demonstrate to all of the employees that quality work is expected.

Giving a single technician the responsibility for reporting damaged, or missing, parts is often the easiest, and most effective, method. The other technicians in the shop will know to go to someone they work with every day to report the problem, and the shop management will have a single person, instead of everyone, letting them know what needs to be repaired or replaced. This practice also gives the responsible individual the opportunity to see the issue for themselves, and sometimes resolve it before it gets to management.

Of course, for any inspection or maintenance program to be effective the shop must take action when it is brought to light that equipment needs repair or replacement. At the very least a timetable should be given the technicians for when the problem will be remedied. Quick action creates a positive environment that will translate into technicians taking better care of your equipment and your customer's vehicles.

Scan Tools

Of all the tools in the shop, the one tool that confounds more repair shop owners is the diagnostic scan tool. Scan tools come with their own unique challenges and have become required equipment for every repair shop. Whether used for diagnostics, computer reprogramming, or even replacing an ignition key, as a shop owner or manager, you will likely need to purchase multiple scan tools.

Something to Consider

You will want to have at least one scan tool for every two or three technicians that you employ. Doing so will ensure continued productivity.

If your goal is to not send a customer that comes to you for diagnosis and repair away from your shop to seek service elsewhere, then you need to make a significant investment in scan tool technology. Scan tools not only make diagnostics easier, but often are required to execute a repair. Compounding the challenge, unlike other tools such as alignment machines that have a long life span, scan tools can become obsolete quickly. Falling behind in your diagnostic capabilities not only hurts your ability to serve customers, but makes it all that much harder to catch up.

Keeping up with scan tool technology and software is a constant challenge for a shop owner or manager. Whether your shop utilizes generic scan tools from a manufacturer such as Snap On, Mac Tools, OTC, or an OE manufacturer scan tool, you are challenged with regular and necessary software updates and subscription services. With the proliferation of computer controlled systems you have no choice but to stay up to date.

You will want to have some sort of scan tool for every two or three technicians in the repair shop – if not each technician. Many technicians today have their own scan tool, but as scan tools are expensive this is sometimes impractical. At the very least, you will want to ensure that work productivity is not slowed by having too few scan tools in the shop. There are not many service procedures today that don't require the use of some sort of scan tool during the diagnostic or repair process.

Working on today's vehicles requires an up-to-date scan tool. Whereas in years past you often would need an OE scan tool, today many scan tools have similar functionality to the OE tool. Whether used for reconfiguring an onboard computer, initializing a specific component function, or active testing components (bi-directional controls) during diagnostics and after a repair, you cannot afford to be without the appropriate scan tool.

Key Point

When purchasing a generic scan tool, have the representative demonstrate the unit to your most qualified technicians and get their input on which tool they like best and why. This will ensure you've purchased a tool that will increase shop productivity.

As advanced computer technology is increasingly used on today's vehicles you will find that many components, relays for instance, that used to be mechanical in nature, are now solid-state components, meaning they have no moving parts and are actually computers.

The challenge here is that many of these components require an OE like scan tool in order to initialize them for proper operation. There are generic scan tools that have the ability to initialize or communicate with components such as these so be sure to invest in one that has this capability.

When choosing a generic scan tool it is best to invite your tool representatives to the shop to perform a demonstration of the capabilities of their particular scan tool while having all of your technicians present for the demonstration. This allows you, the shop owner or manager, to determine which scan tool the majority of your technicians prefer, why they prefer it, and ensure the maximum value for your purchase. Choose a scan tool that has multiple functions such as an easy-to-use oscilloscope function.

As with all shop equipment, proper maintenance, care, and updating of all scan tools is crucial. This is an expense you will need to budget for on a yearly basis. Believe it or not, this expense can represent upwards of $10,000 or more per year. Not maintaining, caring for, or updating diagnostic software will cost your repair shop in productivity, efficiency, and customer satisfaction.

I continue to be amazed at the number of shops that prefer to sublet computer reprogramming to area businesses. So many shops have decided to not purchase OE scan tools, or scan tools with reprogramming capabilities, that I know individuals who now make a living roaming from shop to shop reprogramming newly installed components. Although this is one way to handle the scan tool challenge, and for some shops it makes sense, it can create longer wait times for your customers, and places yet another business and individual in the repair process. A case can be made that it also gives away business.

Key Point

Before purchasing any service information subscriptions, consult with your technicians and determine which they like the best.

Don't be afraid to invest in the equipment to properly execute a complete repair. If information to make a good decision is what you need, you can find it through the internet, speaking with other shop owners, or consulting with a technical training organization. Certain trade organizations can help you obtain information on how other shops handle their scan tool challenges.

If it's expense that keeps you from purchasing another scan tool, then determine for yourself what the ROI is in terms of time based on the mix of vehicles that your shop services. I think you'll find that it's well worth the money to invest in at least one OE manufacturer scan tool.

Key Point

Subletting computer reprogramming is possible, but it slows the repair process and you run the risk of tarnishing customer satisfaction by doing so.

Service Information

All repair shops need access to vehicle service information. This will include wiring diagrams, repair information, diagnostic information, and in some instances parts information. There are many places today, all electronic, to find vehicle repair information. What you choose to utilize for your repair shop in terms of service information subscriptions, should be predicated on input from your technicians, your service writers, and the price you're willing to pay.

Something to Consider

Although generic service information programs are good, there are many reasons to supplement your existing subscriptions with factory service information subscriptions. Faster updating of information is one reason.

AllData, Mitchell, and other electronic services provide – manufacturer-like service information all in one place. Sometimes this information is as good as you read in the OE manufacturer documentation; other times you may find it to be lacking. Most OE manufacturers provide online access to their service information databases on a subscription basis. It is my opinion that OE manufacturer subscriptions are worth investing in. As was the case with scan tool investments, you may want to only purchase OE manufacturer subscription service information from those manufacturers who form the majority of your customer base. I've seen cases where the cost of just one subscription more than paid for itself in the amount of time it saved during the repair. Timely repairs mean happy customers.

Also, like scan tools, the supplier of service information that you choose should be one that the majority of your technicians are comfortable with using. If your technicians are uncomfortable using a particular brand of service information, then it is likely they will waste valuable time trying to find wiring diagrams, service information, or other repair related information.

Something to Consider

Two excellent sources for repair information are:

www.nastf.org

www.iatn.net

Technical Training

Every repair shop should have a plan to provide their technicians with continuing education. This is necessary today because vehicle technology advances so rapidly. The technicians that you hire might, or might not, have a strong technical base upon which they can build new knowledge. This makes it important that you, as the repair shop owner or manager, understand your technician's strengths and weaknesses and develop a training plan. Encourage your technicians to seek out and attend training classes.

Technical training can be acquired through local vocational centers, technical colleges, or independent businesses such as Automotive Aftermarket Training Inc.(AAT), Carquest Technical Institute (CTI), or other organizations. Some technical training is better than others, but any technical training can be better than none. You can find a list of technical training organizations, along with their contact information, in Appendix H.

Something to Consider

Technical training is a must in today's automotive repair industry. Seek out and obtain the best quality training you can find.

If your technicians haven't taken a particular class in two or three years, encourage them to retake that class. Even the most seasoned, veteran technicians, can always learn something from a class on certain basics such as electrical or engine control diagnostics. None of us ever learn all we could have learned in every class we take!

As good an idea as technical training can be, there are often challenges providing technicians with training opportunities. Some technicians will jump at the chance to learn something new or to hone their diagnostic skills, while others will find it to be nothing more than an inconvenience to attend a class or complete online training modules. Technicians that work for independent repair shops are often asked to attend the training on their own time, usually at night after having worked all day. Other training programs are on weekends, again on the technicians own time. This alone can be disincentive for technicians to attend training classes. How can you incentivize technicians to attend training?

Offering to pay your technicians to attend training classes, and providing some sort of dinner before they go (if the class doesn't provide dinner), can sometimes encourage technicians to attend training classes, or at the very least ease the pain they feel. For some technicians it is more than enough for the shop to make them aware of training opportunities and they will make every effort to attend. For other technicians, when it comes to taking classes on their own, they need more incentive to attend. Paying technicians to attend a three or four hour class four times a year will likely pay dividends in customer satisfaction, fixed right first time, and shop efficiency. The shop owner, or manager, attending the class with the technicians is probably the best incentive.

If you have the space and are willing to invest the time, there are custom training programs available that will provide training at your shop. These programs will provide your technicians training in specific areas that they feel they need to improve in. Some shops are willing to schedule around a training class one day a month, or one day a quarter so that technicians can get technical training during the day. This often increases the attention span of the technicians in attendance, allows them to be in an environment that is more comfortable to them than a classroom, and allows them to practice diagnostics or repairs utilizing the same equipment that they use every day. AAT, Inc. (www.intelligentmechanic.com) is one company that provides these services.

Something to Consider

Custom training programs are available at your location. Visit www.rsrcoach.com or www.service-salesacademy.com for more information.

A secondary benefit to providing your technicians with the opportunity for technical training is that it can be used as an employee retention tool. Many technicians, seeing the investment the shop is making in their own professional development, will feel more loyalty and a closer connection to their employer. Attracting new, quality employees is often easier when the individual can see that the employer will be investing in them as well. Presenting technical training as an employment benefit can set your shop apart from other area shops.

Something to Consider

Incentivizing technicians to attend technical training classes is a good idea. Paying a technician to attend training increases the cost to the shop, but will also result in higher attendance and more shop efficiency.

Providing technical training to your technicians will increase customer satisfaction, shop productivity, and increase your employee retention, as well as help to attract quality technicians.

Always Remember

- **New technicians need to be properly trained by someone qualified in all safety, operation and maintenance aspects of shop equipment.**
- **Alignment specifications should be updated at least once every two years.**
- **OE manufacturer scan tools are available for purchase from every OE manufacturer.**
- **OE scan tools have increased functionality over current aftermarket scan tools.**
- **Technical training is a necessity in today's automotive repair industry. Seek out and find quality technical training for your technicians. Incentivize your technicians for attending training.**

Chapter 7: Managing the Shop

In This Chapter

- **Hours of operation.**
- **Alternative production schedules.**
- **Setting labor rates.**

So far we've discussed four important components of any automotive repair shop; the customer, the service writer(s), the technicians, and shop equipment. Each of these areas is important individually, but together they add up to more than the sum of their parts. Now let's discuss how all of this is brought together to produce an exceptional automotive repair business focused on customer retention.

A Focus on the Customer

Every business exists to serve their customers, and high customer retention is what creates a sustainable business. Customer retention is a function of customer satisfaction. Too often we fall into the attitude of "if it wasn't for these customers, things would be great". Attitudes and business practices that do not ultimately serve the customer need to be identified and changed. Often it is these attitudes and practices that are the difference between a good business and an exceptional business.

Key Point

Hours of operation should be structured to suit the customer, not only the repair shop.

Let's take a look at service management from a customer perspective. We've already discussed the customer experience as it relates to the actual visit, but what about before the customer shows up at your shop? When you think about needing to bring your vehicle into the repair shop for service, one of the first considerations you take into account is when is the shop open? How convenient will it be for me to get to the shop, drop my car off, and then return to pick it up? The days and hours of operation in the automotive repair business are too often structured for the convenience of the repair shop rather than the convenience of the customer.

Hours of Operation

If you look around you'll notice dealership service departments beginning to open full hours on Saturday and, as blasphemous as it sounds, all day on Sunday. Some extremely large shops in large metro areas are running multiple shifts. Why is this? Are they just glutens for punishment? Are they trying to put the "little guy" out of business? Are they just plain crazy? You might answer 'yes' to each question, but look at it from a customer perspective.

Something to Consider

Alternative work schedules can provide higher revenue for the shop, while giving employees more time off.

Virtually everyone drives a car, and with only a few exceptions, everyone has to go to work. Customers that work Monday through Friday from 9am to 5pm, plus whatever time it takes for them to commute, sometimes up to an additional three hours a day, do not often find it convenient during the week to bring their vehicle in for service. Even if a loaner car or shuttle service were available, they still may not find it convenient due to the time at which they are required to pick up or drop off their vehicle. That leaves two days of the week

---

Key Point

Being open weekends can be very productive for repair shops. These are the days that customers are better able to bring their vehicles to the shop for service or repair.

---

when customers don't have their schedule restricted by something like work. It is these two days when they may more conveniently be able to drop off or pick up their vehicle. This is the reason for being open on Saturday and Sunday.

These two days, in many instances, can be a repair shop's *most productive* two days of the week. Customers have time to bring the vehicle to the repair shop, customers may be more likely to drop their vehicle off at the repair shop rather than wait for it, and customers are generally feeling less pressured and are more willing to purchase additional services and repairs.

Key Point

Many organizations are moving to alternative work schedules to increase efficiency and productivity.

Now nobody wants to work seven days a week. If you are a small repair shop you likely won't have a choice as to how many days a week you can be open. You need to balance employee satisfaction with customer satisfaction. If you're the sole owner of the repair shop and a technician yourself, then you may not be able to be open more than five days a week. If, however, you are a larger repair shop who employs a number of technicians, then you have some terrific options.

Another concern might be what reaction your technicians will have the first time you mention the shop will be open all day Saturday or Sunday! So how do you open on weekends, often the most convenient time for customers to visit your shop, and avoid working seven days a week? The answer is an alternative work schedule.

The 4/10 Production Schedule

Examine your current shop hours. Is your shop open now from seven in the morning until six at night? If so, of those hours, how many are your technicians working? Some of you may answer nine out of those hours, some may have answered all of those hours, or some may have answered somewhere in between. I know very few technicians who only work eight hour days in reality.

```
                    Key Point

    See the sample schedule for how the 4/10 work sched-
    ule is laid out. You can get easy tools from the internet
    to make scheduling your technicians and service writ-
                      ers easier.
```

I would make the case that were you to be open those 11 hours from seven in the morning until six at night and your technicians were to work those hours productively, you could arrange your shop schedule so that your technicians could have three days off each week while your repair shop is open six full days a week.

This schedule arrangement is known as the 4/10 schedule. It means that technicians will work four ten hour days each week. Each technician gets three days a week off, and every three weeks each technician gets five days off in a row. This can greatly increase employee satisfaction! The shop gets to fully staff the work bays six full days each week, gets to earn an extra days revenue every week, and gets the reputation of being a great place to work!

Let's look at a sample schedule. This is a schedule for a repair shop that has six work bays. To accommodate the work schedule they've hired an additional three technicians. The additional technicians allowed them to create three teams of three technicians each.

Notice that each team rotates the day off schedule, with each team getting five straight days off every three weeks. This allows the shop to fully staff each work bay with a technician, and do so six days each week.

Yes, this means that some technicians must share a bay, and must be able to roll their toolbox, but this is a small price to pay for the increased production. In my experience, once technicians try this new schedule and work through some of the logistic and communication bugs that always come up, they grow to really like it.

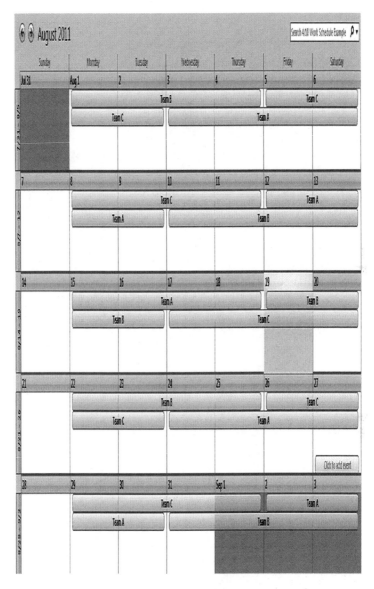

If the scheduling seems daunting for you, have no fear. Many shop management software programs can help with employee scheduling as well. If your shop management software doesn't have the ability to help with scheduling, there are online resources that can be purchased for a onetime fee that will allow you to plug in your teams and it will create the schedule for you.

Change is hard for all of us. We like what we are used to, and technicians may be challenged by a new work schedule at first. Explain the reasoning and benefits behind this type of schedule and solicit your technician's input. Once they, and their families, get used to the rotating schedule, they will recognize the benefits of increased time off and a more productive work schedule.

This schedule allows you to give your employees more time off, allows the shop to stay open longer hours, and to be open hours your customers find convenient. To me that's a win, win, win solution!

Something to Consider

Your labor rate will dictate the type of customer you attract.

Labor Rates

Labor rates are an aspect some shop owners struggle with. Customers love low labor rates. Shop owners love high labor rates. The right labor rate must fall somewhere in between. Setting an appropriate labor rate isn't always as simple as it seems. Your labor rate sends a message to the market.

You, as a shop owner, need to decide what your market will bear, what portion of the market you are interested in serving, and what your business realities and goals are. A lower labor rate will attract a very different customer than a mid-range or high labor rate will.

Key Point

Do a yearly analysis of your labor rate to make sure that you are in line with where you want to be.

Not only will you attract a different customer, but the kind of customer you attract will dictate where you will source your parts, what level of customer service you will offer, what the customer expectations will be, and will even dictate the appearance of your facility. In some instances, geographical location alone dictates the kind of customer you need to attract. In other cases you will have a choice as to which part of the market you wish to serve.

Begin by looking around your local area and see what your competitors are charging for their labor rates. Notice what kind of customers they seem to be attracting. You can get an idea of what your competition is doing by "mystery shopping" your competitors over the phone, visiting your competitors in person, or sometimes trade organizations will track this data for you. No matter how you gather labor rate information on your competitors you will want to also note how busy they are. Have they priced themselves out of the market? What kind of vehicles are in the shop or parking lot? Do they appear to be serving the same customer you are trying to attract?

Your labor rate also has to reflect your quality of work. It does you no good to set a high labor rate, attract the kind of customer that is willing to pay a high labor rate, and then turn out poor quality work. That combination will likely have a negative effect on your business.

Remember, setting a low labor rate will send a certain message, and attract a certain customer. Setting a high labor rate will send the opposite message and will likely attract the customer that is expecting high quality work, and an over-the-top service experience. It's up to you as a shop owner to decide where you want to be.

Quality Control

YOU HAVE NOTHING IF YOU DON'T HAVE QUALTIY WORKMANSHIP. Never forget this. This is so important that I'll mention it again in the Marketing chapter.

Implementing a Quality Control Process is about protecting your ability to increase Gross Profit in the long-term. Yes, in the short-term it can save you some pain, but it is more about never letting anything get in the way of Customer Trust.

Quality Control Programs look different in different shops. Often the biggest challenge is finding that single person who can be responsible for Quality Control in any given shop. Although the qualifications are not "over the top", finding someone who can commit to QC on a full-time basis and not cost the shop a lot of money in payroll can be a challenge.

Shops who are big enough to have a Shop Foreman, will put that person in charge of QC. Other shops will hire a "retired" shop owner or the like to run the QC program. Small shops who don't have the benefit of either will sometimes use Service Advisors. I've even set up QC Buddies to check each other's work in shops who just didn't have the personnel.

No matter what type of QC system you set up, the most important thing is that you create one. Here is what I believe a QC Process should look like:

- Technician ultimately responsible for doing quality work and is held accountable.

- Second set of eyes on the vehicle – whether a "buddy" or a formal QC Foreman.

- Road test where practical – always.

- Second person signs off that the vehicle was inspected – signatures create accountability.

Here's part of the reason I strongly believe in QC – if you buy a $25 pair of jeans at a big box store it comes with a piece of paper in the pocket that says "Inspected By". Shouldn't a $1200 repair be "Inspected By"? A good QC program can be marketed to your customers as a value add (even if other shops have a QC program, almost nobody promotes the fact that they do).

The other reason I believe in formal QC Programs is that we are all human. Every technician has made a mistake or forgotten something. I want your shop to catch the mistake before your customer discovers it. Even the smallest, simplest, jobs can create a mistake that leads to customer dissatisfaction. Think about a customer's reaction to a Maintenance Reminder Light being left on – for you, it's just a light. For the customer it means you didn't do the work! Even the smallest mistake leads to a negative perception.

Implement and enforce a quality control program in your shop today. You'll be glad you did.

Always Remember

- **Customer convenience is key to growing customer retention.**
- **Customer retention makes a business money.**
- **Alternative work schedules allow a shop to be open longer hours, more days of the week and realize higher revenue.**
- **Alternative work schedules allow technicians to make a regular paycheck, while having more time off for themselves and their families.**
- **Labor rates say more about your shop than just how much you charge to repair vehicles.**
- **You have nothing if you don't have quality workmanship - consistently.**

Chapter 8: Financial Management

In This Chapter

- **Financial Analysis.**
- **Reading a balance sheet.**
- **Reading a cash flow statement.**
- **Reading and Income statement.**

A book on managing an automotive service facility is not complete without a discussion regarding the financial aspects of automotive service. Most shop owners and managers went into the automotive business because they were good at fixing cars and wanted the independence of owning their own repair shop, not because they wanted to be an accountant. As a result, for many shop owners accounting and financial management is an area that gets neglected.

As long as the bills are paid, customers pay up before taking their vehicle, and there's some money left over at the end of the month, then all is good. However if you're truly interested in growing your business you need to pay attention to the financial aspects of your operation. Much like the diagnostic data we access when making a repair attempt on a vehicle, your financial statements will show you areas of improvement, serve to raise warnings of bad things to come, and allow you to make choices about how to operate your business.

Key Point

You don't have to be a "numbers person" to understand your financial statements.

In this chapter we will discuss the basics of reading the core financial statements - the Balance Sheet, the Cash Flow Statement, and the Income Statement. You don't have to be a financial genius to understand the numbers and how they relate to the operation of your business. You can make financial analysis as simple, or as complicated as you want to. This is also not intended to be a complete discussion on the financial aspects of your business. The intent of this section is to get you started down the road of financial analysis. If at some point you want to know more, contact a certified accounting professional and explain to them your goals in understanding financial statements.

The following also assumes that you either have some knowledge of bookkeeping, or employ the services of a professional bookkeeper or accountant.

The Balance Sheet

A balance sheet shows assets and liabilities, essentially the value of what you own and the balance of what you owe. Much like a data list snap shot, a balance sheet is a snapshot of your business at one point in time.

Key Point

The balance sheet is a snapshot of what you own and what you owe at one moment in time.

The following is a sample Balance Sheet.

John's Advanced Auto Service

Balance Sheet

	2010	2011		2010	2011
ASSETS			*LIABILITIES AND STOCKHOLDERS' EQUITY*		
			Current Liabilities		
Current Assets			Wages Payable	$0	$0
Cash	$23,597	$24,538	Accounts Payable	34,893	35,871
Marketable Securities	0	0	Taxes Payable	1,283	894
Accounts Receivable,			Other	35,981	42,198
Net of Uncollectible			Total Current		
Accounts	2000	150	Liabilities	$72,157	$78,963
Inventory	15000	12657	Long-Term Liabilities		
Other	0	0	Mortgage Payable	$98,327	$85,612
Prepaid Expenses	0	0	Bond Payable	0	0
Total Current Assets	$40,597	$37,345	Deferred Taxes	0	0
			Other	0	0
Fixed Assets			Total Long-Term		
Buildings and Equipment	$150,826	$134,792	Liabilities	$98,327	$85,612
Less Accumulated			Stockholders' Equity		
Depreciation	6297	2746	Common Stock, $X Par	$0	$0
Net Buildings and			Com. Stock-Excess		
Equipment	$144,529	$132,046	over par	0	0
Land	0	0	Preferred Stock, X%,		
Other	4675	7824	$X Par, X shares	0	0
Total Fixed Assets	$149,204	$139,870	Retained Earnings	26,808	21,324
			Total Stockholders'	$26,808	$21,324
Goodwill	0	358	Equity		
Other	7491	8326	TOTAL LIABILITIES		
			& STOCKHOLDERS'		
TOTAL ASSETS	$197,292	$185,899	EQUITY	$197,292	$185,899

Service Management Made Simple

Key Point

The IRS usually sets the minimum number of years an asset is expected to last. Your accountant can help you determine how much depreciation to account for.

On the left-hand side, the balance sheet lists everything the business owns, such as cash, accounts receivable (what customers owe on account), and fixed assets such as buildings and equipment. On the right-hand side is a list of everything the business owes such as accounts payable (payments due to vendors) and the remaining balance of loans payable. The difference between the total assets and the total liabilities is a known as "equity". While some think that "equity" represents the value of a business, the reality is that "equity" is purely a calculation and doesn't really mean anything from an accounting perspective.

Something to Consider

All equipment and buildings will depreciate over time. Be sure to account for the depreciation appropriately.

Assets represent anything of value the business owns. They are broken into two categories – current assets and long-term assets. Current assets include cash and anything that can be converted into cash in less than a year. In the example balance sheet you can see that this includes cash, accounts receivable, and any inventory the shop may have on hand. The assumption is that your customers will pay you what they owe you in less than a year and that you will sell any inventory that you currently own within a year. Please note that this is only an assumption, you may actually have parts that you bought five years ago and may not sell for another five years. But you do have the intent of selling the parts and that's what's important!

The fixed assets portion of the balance sheet contains physical things that you own such as land, buildings, and equipment items that are expected to last and be used over several years. Fixed assets are reported on the Balance Sheet at their original cost less depreciation. Depreciation is a way of reporting the expected loss of value over time. The Internal

> **Key Point**
>
> The difference between total assets and total liabilities is known as "equity".

Revenue Service (IRS) usually sets the minimum number of years an asset is expected to last. For example, let's say you purchased a diagnostic machine for $7,000. The IRS says that most equipment should last 7 years. So the yearly depreciation on the diagnostic machine would be $1,000 a year ($7,000 divided by $1,000). When the diagnostic machine is purchased it would show up on the Balance Sheet as an asset worth $7,000. At the end of the first year of using the asset, you would record depreciation of $1,000. The asset would now appear on the Balance Sheet at $6,000 ($7,000 minus $1,000). Land, in general, will appreciate, while buildings and equipment will depreciate through use. Your accountant can help you determine the correct depreciation number for your equipment and facilities.

Key Point

Balance sheets can be created monthly, quarterly, or yearly.

Goodwill is a portion of money paid over the estimated price of acquiring a business or service. This is sometimes referred to as "blue sky money" in the automotive industry. Generally you will only include this number when you have made the purchase of another business and have included it in your current operations (rather than account for it separately or hold it as part of another corporation).

Liabilities include anything you owe to others related to the operation of the business. It can be money that you've borrowed to finance the business, money you haven't yet paid to employees or suppliers, and money that is owed to stock holders. As you can see, the balance sheet is like a scan tool data list snap shot of what you own and what you owe in your business. It is rather general in nature, but gives an indication of how much money is being taken in, what the physical assets are worth, and how much money is owed to various entities. Balance sheets can be created monthly, quarterly, or yearly depending on how often you want to see the "big picture" of your business.

Income Statement

The second financial document that you will want to be familiar with is the Income Statement, or Profit and Loss Statement. This is a document that describes a business's performance over a period of time. Unlike the balance sheet that was a snapshot of assets and liabilities at one point in time, the income statement provides more detailed information over a longer period of time – it could be a month, a quarter, or a year. Essentially the income statement records how much money was earned (revenue), how much was spent (expenses), and what was left over (net income or net profit) during a specified period of time.

Key Point

The Income Statement shows the operation of the business over a longer period of time than a Balance Sheet does.

It is from the income statement that you will determine values such as Gross Profit, Gross Profit Percentage, Cost of Goods Sold, General & Accounting Expense, Personnel Expense, etc.. The income statement is a useful tool in running your business as it allows you to compare your actual business income and expenses to your projected income and expenses (Pro Forma). You can also perform useful analysis of your income statement utilizing certain ratios.

On the following page you can see an example of an income statement:

John's Advanced Auto Service

Statement of Income

For the Years Ending June 30,2010 and June 30,2011

		2010		2011
Revenues	$	862,578.00	$	901,892.00
Less Cost of Goods Sold	$	150,789.00	$	178,459.00
Gross Profit	$	711,789.00	$	723,433.00
Operating Expenses	$	56,721.00	$	43,581.00
Selling Expenses	$	22,457.00	$	21,897.00
Other	$	6,879.00	$	5,998.00
General Expenses	$	37,589.00	$	26,802.00
Administrative Expenses	$	44,789.00	$	49,012.00
Total Operating Expenses	$	111,714.00	$	147,290.00
Operating Income	$	600,075.00	$	576,143.00
Interest Expense	$	3,893.00	$	5,498.00
Income Before Taxes	$	596,182.00	$	570,645.00
Income Taxes	$	60,932.00	$	59,781.00
Net Income	$	535,250.00	$	510,864.00

Keep in mind when reviewing this statement of income that it can be created to be as complex or as simple as you choose it to be. I personally prefer a statement that is slightly more complex than the example given here. I would like to see the Operating Expense, Cost of Goods Sold, and General Expenses lines broken down further. This is because I come from a small business background where I'm very close to those things that affect these lines. In larger companies it may be enough to know that these are the areas that have contributed to the overall profit or loss of the company.

Further analysis can be done with the income statement as well by turning it into percentages. For instance you can calculate gross profit as percent of sales, or G&A expenses (General Expenses) as a percent of sales. Really you could calculate any percent of sale value that you thought might be useful to you. Many times you can find trade organizations that can provide you with guidelines for what your percent-of-sale numbers should be, based on the industry.

Something to Consider

You can calculate any percent of sale value that you might find useful to your specific operation.

In general, I like to look at gross profit as a percent of revenues, and various expenses expressed as a percent of revenue. Gross Profit represents the amount of direct profit you make by selling something. For example, the gross profit on an oil change would be the difference between the sales price of the oil change less the cost of materials (replacement oil, a new oil filter, etc.) and labor (the cost of paying an employee to complete the oil change). The higher your gross profit, the more profitable your business is likely to be. Obviously, the lower your expenses as a percent of revenues are, the better off your business is.

Although different businesses will suggest different figures, usually anything above a gross profit percentage of 50% is considered to be good. Normally you'll want to see this upwards of 65% in the automotive service industry.

One of the best ways to see how you are doing is to prepare a budget, also known as a Pro Forma. This is essentially the same thing as the income, or profit and loss statement, but is a guesstimate of what will happen in the future. A budget should be your best guess as to what will happen with your revenues and expenses for the coming year. As the new year progresses you can see how you are doing compared to how you thought you would be doing. This comparison of budget to actual results will let you know if you are on track, ahead of the game, or maybe in trouble. You can also use your

budget to see what might happen if you made changes in your operations. What would the budget look like if you added another technician, or opened a second location? By creating a copy of your income statement and then plugging in various numbers you can see how the different revenues and expenses affect your net income. This can be a useful tool when you are trying to grow your business, not to mention that it can be fun!

Create a Pro Forma document using a spreadsheet program, plug in whatever numbers you want, and see how the bottom line is affected. Once you get a set of "working" values in terms of your revenues and expenses, see if you can accomplish those goals with your business. Compare your pro forma with your actual income statement on a monthly or quarterly basis. Over time you'll learn a lot about what drives your business.

Cash Flow Statement

Another aspect of financial analysis you will want to be familiar with is the Cash Flow Statement. Cash flow is something that small businesses are very close to. As such, you may not currently prepare a Cash Flow Statement, but instead have a "feel" for where money is coming in and where your money is being spent. If this is the case, you will want to prepare a detailed Cash Flow Statement that can quantify what you already "know". You may be surprised at what you learn when you see the actual numbers laid out before you!

Key Point

Use a Pro Forma to set financial goals for your business and then track them throughout the year.

This document is prepared in more detail than the balance sheet, and will show exactly where and how money comes to your business, and how it leaves your business. Another way of considering the Cash Flow Statement is that it shows you exactly how, and why, the changes in your cash occurred over the period it was prepared for.

The following page contains an example of a cash flow statement:

John's Advanced Auto Service

Statement of Cash Flows

For the Years Ending June 30,2010 and June 30,2011

Cash Flows from Operating Activities

Collections from Customers	$651,783
Payments to Suppliers	-243784
Payments to Employees	-190417
Reduction in Accounts Receivable	5691
Increase in Accounts Receivable	0
Increase in Accounts Payable	2537
Decrease in Accounts Payable	-2567
Increase in Inventory	-45891
Ammortization of Goodwill	0
Other	0
Net Cash from Operating Activities	$177,352

Cash Flows from Investing Activities

Purchase of New Equipment	-$55,786
Other	-53,596
Net Cash Used for Investing Activities	-$109,382

Cash Flows from Financing Activities

Borrowing from Creditors	$23,568
Issuance of Stock	0
Payment of Dividends	0
Other	0
Net Cash from Financing Activities	$23,568

NET INCREASE/(DECREASE) IN CASH	$91,538
CASH, BEGINNING OF YEAR	78923
CASH, END OF YEAR	$170,461

When taking a look at the example cash flow statement, keep in mind that yours may look slightly different. Differences in how you, or your accountant, set up your accounts may dictate what lines appear on your cash flow statement. You may want to make this statement more or less detailed, depending on the aspects of your business that you wish to keep a close eye on. The bottom line is this: money coming into the business will be recorded as positive, and money leaving will be recorded as negative.

In the example you can see that we start with cash coming in from your customers. From this number we add anything that can be considered an increase in cash such as a reduction in accounts receivable (money that was paid the business), an increase in accounts payable (money the business owes, but hasn't paid out yet thus making it positive), any increase in goodwill (or "blue sky"), and any other money coming in from other revenue sources or financing of the business (borrowed money).

We then subtract all the money paid out. This can be money paid for supplies, an increase in money we paid for more inventory, money for equipment, and money that we paid the employees. Any money that left the business is recorded as a negative value. These changes are then tabulated and subtracted or added to the amount of cash on hand at the end of the previous period to give a net increase, or decrease in cash.

Your cash flow statement will give you an idea of where exactly money is coming to your business and where it is leaving your business.

Other Terms

Here are some other financial terms that you should become familiar with:

Accounts Receivable

This line on a statement represents the money that is owed to a company by customers or others who have purchased goods or services. Accounts receivable is considered an asset.

Accounts Payable

This line represents money owed by a business to suppliers or short term creditors. Accounts payable is considered a liability.

LIFO

Last In First Out (LIFO) is an accounting term relating to the keeping of inventory. This accounting method associates cost of goods sold with the latest in inventory purchases.

FIFO

First In First Out (FIFO) is an accounting term that also relates to a method of accounting for inventory. Unlike LIFO, it associates the cost of goods sold to the oldest inventory purchases (the first purchased).

Chart of Accounts

This is how your accountant will categorize your income and expense accounts. Categories are usually defined by a general account number, and then broken down into specifics within that group.

For example:

Revenue:	4000
Revenue from tire sales:	4001
Revenue from maintenance sales:	4002
Revenue from parts sales:	4003
Revenue from general repair:	4004

Fixed Costs

This line will often appear on your income statement and Pro Forma. Fixed costs relate to those costs that do not vary based on your sales or production volume. Examples of fixed costs might be mortgage payments, salaries, certain utilities, or some professional services like cleaning.

Variable Costs

Variable costs will also appear on your income statement and pro forma documents. These are costs or expenses that will change with increased or decreased production and sales levels. Examples of these might be personnel expense (depending on your pay plans), certain utilities, supplies, or maintenance items.

Always Remember

- **Paying attention to financial reports can quantify aspects of your business that you may not be fully aware of.**
- **The balance sheet gives you a snapshot view of your finances at one point in time.**
- **The cash flow statement allows a shop owner or manager to identify exactly where money is coming into the business and leaving the business.**
- **The income statement gives you a good idea of where money is being spent, and where income is coming from over a longer period of time.**
- **Further financial analysis can be done utilizing the income statement and various financial ratios.**

Chapter 9: Performance Indicators

In This Chapter

- **Key Performance Indicators.**
- **Knowing what to pay attention to.**
- **Understanding where money is made.**

When I first wrote this book I intentionally chose to not focus on the numbers. To me, if you focus on people, both your customers and your employees, and can do a better job in that area than your competition, then you will succeed. The numbers should follow great customer service and strong employee retention. I still feel that way, however there are shops in the industry who have the people aspect nailed down and now need more. There are also readers of this book who want to expand their knowledge with the hope of moving onward and upward. Numbers are important to every business as they are indicators of many things. Certainly, understand the numbers, but don't get too deep and forget about the people part of the business.

In this chapter, I will introduce some Key Performance Indicators. These KPI's, as they are known, are those calculations that will tell you how your business is doing. Is it likely to be making money? How does it compare with industry standards that have been proven over time? Is there discounting being done by service advisors that is taking money away from the business? Do technicians work as hard as they say they do? Yes, you can tell all of this from some numbers.

Using Key Performance Indicators

Before we get into the numbers let me say this: your numbers are only as good as your data. We can make numbers say anything we want by using the numbers we like in the calculations. We can also get numbers that look really good by

---

Key Point

Use the KPI calculator on the Repair Shop Rescue app to quickly calculate basic KPI's and see where you stand today, this week, or this month! The numbers will help you understand and grow your business.

---

using bad data collection practices (or get numbers that look bad, when they actually are not). Understand where the number is coming from before you put too much faith in a KPI. If service counter, or technician, practices don't allow our service management system to collect accurate data on how much time a technician spent on a particular job, then your production KPI is not going to be accurate. If your technicians don't punch in and out at the beginning or end of the day, you won't be able to calculate productivity. If you service management system uses a different definition of productivity than we do here, the numbers won't make sense to you, or you'll make decisions based on inaccurate knowledge.

Something to Consider

Knowing where the numbers come from and ensuring their accuracy is critical to properly using KPI's to grow and manage your business.

When you talk about KPI's with anyone in the industry you'd better first define exactly what you are talking about and how it is being calculated. A major frustration of mine about the automotive industry is that we have yet to define some basic terms in such a way that we can all speak a common language. You will also discover over time that everyone has a set of numbers that they will tell you are the most important. This is more subjective than objective in most cases. Find the numbers that you believe drive your particular business, make sure the data collected is accurate, and pay attention to them on a weekly or monthly basis.

Properly using KPI's to run your business is more than just seeing a number and comparing it to a standard. You must understand what data you want, what data is being collected, the accuracy of the data being collected, how the calculation is being made, and then how to influence the process to improve the number!

The Key Performance Indicators

Here is a list of the KPI's you should learn to calculate and understand what they mean:

- Effective Labor Rate

- Average Repair Order Dollars

- Average Repair Order Hours

- Technician Productivity %

- Technician Efficiency %

- Scheduling Efficiency

- Total Revenue

- Gross Profit per Job %

- Net Profit %

- RO's per Service Advisor

This isn't a comprehensive list of all the industry KPI's you could possibly calculate. However, get good at knowing and tracking the numbers from this list and understand your financial statement, and you'll have a well-run business! We'll discuss each measurement in the follow pages, although not in any order. They are all important and you may choose to focus on any one of them at any point in time.

Effective Labor Rate

Effective Labor Rate (ELR) is a measurement of how much of your posted labor rate you are actually collecting. As you know, every automotive repair shop has a labor rate. Many have multiple labor rates for various customers (retail, fleet, wholesale, etc.) or for different services (maintenance services may have reduced labor rate to keep costs down or because they can be done quickly). We would all like to think that just because we say we charge $100 per hour labor, that we are collecting $100 per hour on every job. The reality is that due to a number of factors, we don't collect all of that money. Giving customers discounts, not tracking or collecting for diagnostic time, improperly tracking or estimating labor times all have the effect of reducing what we collect for a labor rate.

Key Point

Effective Labor Rate is a metric that will help you ensure you are collecting the amount of money you should be for the labor you perform.

There are two different ways of calculating ELR, depending on what you are looking for. Remember, many of these KPI's can be used for diagnosing a problem. ELR is what I would consider a diagnostic KPI.

The goal with ELR is to have it be as close to your actual labor rate as possible. It should never be less than 90% of your posted rate, and in theory should be 100% of your rate.

One way of calculating ELR is:

Effective Labor Rate = Labor Dollars ÷ Labor Hours

This calculation will tell you if the shop, as a whole, is collecting the labor rate you say you are. In other words, using these numbers will tell you if there is any discounting going on at the service counter.

Something to Consider

Labor dollars are where the shop makes its highest gross profit, therefore ensuring your Effective Labor Rate is as close to your posted labor rate as possible is very important.

The Labor Dollars number comes from your service management system (SMS) as does the Labor Hours. The system tracks this based on what you bill the customer. These are both totals for any given amount of time. You would want to look at these numbers for a period of time such as a week, month, quarter, or even year.

Again, this number tells you how much discounting is going on during that time period. For example, let's say that last week we collected $20,000 in labor and our SMS says we billed 250 hours of work. Our posted labor rate for general repairs is $100 per hour. The calculation then suggests that we have an ELR of $80 per hour. In theory, we should have collected $25,000 in labor dollars! For some reason, we missed out on collecting $5000 dollars in just one week! What could have happened? To find out we would need to audit the repair orders from last week. For some reason we are not charging enough labor for each hour of work. It is unlikely the labor times are inaccurate. More likely either the wrong labor rate was being used for some reason, or the repair order total was being discounted. Looking through even a sample of the repair orders from last week would tell us what happened. Once we know how this is happening, then we can council the service counter employees on how to keep this from happening again.

A second ELR calculation that can be made is this:

ELR = Labor Dollars ÷ Labor Hours Paid Technicians

This calculation works in conjunction with our first calculation and is to be used for diagnosing a discrepancy in collecting labor hours. It is possible that we are not collecting for as many labor hours as we are paying technicians. In this case we are not charging the customer for all the labor we performed. Commonly this is due diagnostic time not being accurately accounted for. This is a problem since the money we make in the repair industry comes from selling time (hours).

Key Point

Effective Labor Rate can be used to identify excessive discounting going on at the service counter, or poor selling of diagnostic time.

It is also possible that we are collecting for more labor hours than we are paying technicians. Although this scenario is less likely, and doesn't necessarily cost us money, it does indicate a disconnect in our processes and needs to be addressed. Understanding Effective Labor Rate will help you to know if you are collecting all of the money you are due for performing labor services or if your employees are giving some away!

Average Repair Order Dollars (ARO)

ARO is a commonly talked about metric in the automotive repair industry. It represents how much money, on average, each repair order you write represents. Since repair order dollars are a combination of parts and labor, this number essentially represents the amount of work you sell each customer. If the number is too low, you aren't selling enough work, or the right kind of work, and you won't make much money. If the number is too high you may be "burning out" your customers (selling them too much work and forcing them to think about going somewhere else).

Key Point

Average Repair Order dollars is probably the most talked about KPI in the industry. Too low and you're not making enough money, too high and you're losing customers.

Your ARO will be different from a shop with a different market, or a shop that focuses on a different type of work (foreign auto repair vs domestic vs heavy truck, etc.). There is no right or wrong answer for what your Average Repair Order Dollars should be. In general, assuming you do mostly car and truck repair and maintenance service it should be greater than $325 and less than $450. If you are working on a large number of fleet vehicles, heavy trucks, or RV's then you can expect a good ARO to be above $450 and likely in the range of $550.

Something to Consider

Unless you perform work on fleet vehicles, heavy duty trucks, or RV's, your ARO should be less than $450 to keep from pushing customers away.

If you are a general repair facility, or dealership service center, and your ARO is less than $325 you will need to examine the types of jobs you primarily do. Your SMS can show you a report than gives the types of work you are doing. If this report shows you are doing a large number of oil changes, light maintenance, tires, and other lesser paying work you will need to examine your courtesy inspection and sales process. A low ARO can be brought up by doing a better job with your Courtesy Inspections and selling. Just focusing on alignments, brake inspections, or undercar components (shocks, struts, suspension, etc.) will bring the ARO up to a more acceptable level for making money.

If you suspect your ARO is too high, you will want to audit a sample of repair orders. This can be done by selecting 50 repair orders written during the time period you are examining the ARO for and looking through them for what types of work was done. You might find that someone was great at upselling, there were a number of big engine jobs, or it was just a run of customers who needed to keep their vehicle on the road. As mentioned previously, the only problem with a high ARO is that you might be discouraging customers and gaining the reputation of being expensive. I suggest backing off the selling a little and working to get more customer visits rather than more money during a single visit. This allows the customer the perception that the vehicle still needs work, but that you are fair with what you charge and are helping them to budget for repairs.

Watch your ARO on a weekly or monthly basis and make sure it stays within an acceptable range. Don't forget, you can also watch ARO by service advisor as well to set individual targets or get a new hire up to speed more quickly.

Average Repair Order Hours

Repair order hours are not tracked as a KPI as much in the industry as I think maybe they should be. I've made the point previously, and will continue to make the point, that we sell labor hours in the automotive repair industry. It's true that the more parts we sell, the more labor hours we are likely to sell, however the gross profit is much lower on parts than it is on labor hours. When I'm working with a shop to grow their business I often will focus service advisors on how many labor hours they sell in a day.

An increase of just 0.5 labor hours per repair order can mean an increase in total revenue for the shop of more than $100,000 per year.

There is no guide for what you Average Repair Order Labor Hours should be. Use this metric to establish a starting point for where you are currently and set a target for where you want to be. Strive for small increases over short periods of time rather than large increases over large amounts of time to avoid the temptation to begin overselling and discouraging customers. Often times in increases in labor hours per RO can come from better accounting for diagnostic time, better selling of diagnostic time, simple services such as battery testing, free alignment checks, headlight restoration, etc.

Technician Productivity %

This should be one of your most watched KPI's in my opinion. It goes with my earlier statements about the fact we sell labor in the repair industry. Technician productivity is how you will make money. Too little productivity and you will leave too much money on the table. There really is no such thing as too much productivity as long as you maintain quality workmanship.

This is one of those KPI's that we must define exactly what we are talking about and calculating. Many times what I describe as productivity, others describe as efficiency. When I talk about Productivity % I'm describing a comparison of the number of *billable hours* a technician produced for the shop each day to the number of hours her or she physically *worked*.

The theory is that if a technician is at work 8 hours each day, they should at least give us 8 hours of billable time each day. If they are not, then we are paying them for hours we cannot collect. The actual percentage will vary from individual to individual, and shop to shop depending on skill level, motivation, shop layout, equipment, etc. This number can be calculated both for individuals and for the shop as a whole. The calculations goes like this:

Technician (or shop) Production % = Billable Hours Produced ÷ Hours Worked x 100

Here's an example:

John worked at total of 42 hours last week based on his time clock hours. The Service Management System shows that he produced 35 billable hours for the shop. Therefore his Technician Productivity % is 35 hours ÷ 42 hours x 100 or 83%.

During the same week, Sara worked 39 total hours and produced 43 billable hours for the shop. Her Productivity % is 39 hours ÷ 42 hours x 100 or 107%.

Opinions vary on what the standard for Productivity % should be. In the dealership world, manufacturers set the standard at 110% or higher depending on the manufacturer. (The standard can be as high as 120% for some OE's).

Independent repair shops will usually see lower productivity. I suggest that the minimum target should be set at 100%. I think that it is a fair expectation for an average technician to be able to give me at least 40 hours in return for being paid 40 hours (of course this goes back to our pay plan discussion from Chapter 5). For most technicians, I expect at least 80% production from them depending on how the shop is laid out, what extra responsibilities they may have or the type of work being performed. Don't let anyone tell you an independent shop can't average higher than 100%. I've seen multiple clients of mine above 100% in total shop productivity. It can be done.

An accurate value for this KPI depends on the ability to accurately track hours worked (time clock) and billable hours (punching on and off each job). This calculation is less dependent on accuracy of individual job punches as the Efficiency % KPI is however. At the very least make sure your

---

Something to Consider

An accurate value for this KPI depends on the ability to accurately track hours worked (time clock) and billable hours (punching on and off each job).

---

employees are punching on and off when the begin work, take breaks, and leave for the day.

I encourage every shop to track this KPI weekly. Track each technician's daily billable hours on a whiteboard that they can see in their regular travels through the shop. This will create a bit of subconscious competition among the technicians and will help push production up each week. Once per week calculate the actual % for each individual as well as the shop total. Set targets, talk about goals, and watch your total revenue improve!

Technician Efficiency %

The Technician Efficiency % KPI is one that is often referred to as Production Efficiency or vice versa. Technician Efficiency is certainly a lot like Production % however it is more of a diagnostic tool if productivity is off and you cannot find a reason for it to be so. Technician Efficiency is a comparison of how much time a technician takes to do a specific job, compared to how many hours the job can be billed for. Think of Production % as daily, or weekly, while Efficiency % is per job.

Here's the formula;

Tech Efficiency % = Hours Billed ÷ Actual Hours x 100

The key in using this metric for diagnosis is in being able to accurately track the actual time the technician took to do the job. If he or she is able to log into and out of the job via tablet or smartphone it sometimes makes the metric more accurate. Punching on or off the job with a time clock or computer will not negate the use of this KPI however.

If you find that a technician is under 90% efficient when using this indicator, look for issues with skill sets, tools and equipment, layout of the bay, or lack of experience. If the efficiency number is always low on just one type of job, then it's usually an easy fix, however when it is consistently low with every job, it may be a training issue, motivation challenge, or mentoring situation.

The reality surrounding this particular KPI is that you won't use it all that much. If you focus on Productivity % and have the right pay plan in place, you just won't need to use it. In case you do, it's good to know how to however.

Scheduling Efficiency %

This indicator works hand in hand with your scheduling system. Unfortunately, many shops never get fine-tuned enough to need it. If you are truly trying to maximize the number of hours you schedule each week, then you'll find this KPI quick and handy. The calculation is exactly what it sounds like – a comparison of the number of hours scheduled to the number of hours available to be scheduled. You might also call this schedule utilization.

Something to Consider

Scheduling Efficiency is an easy metric to track and keeps service counter personnel focused on maximizing the schedule instead of how much work the schedule represents to them.

The reason you might want to utilize this KPI is to encourage your team to schedule as much work as they can. Everyone will have an excuse as to why they don't want to schedule, or won't schedule work. As was stated in Chapter 2 though, efficient scheduling maximizes the amount of work that can be brought into the shop. Staying focused on a metric will sometimes help keep focus away from the amount of service counter work that all those scheduled hours represent. Too often our service counter personnel begin to back off when they see a schedule begin to fill. Their hesitation is always "what if...?" Don't let this hold your organization back! Use the schedule efficiency metric to help fill your bays with work.

Here's an example:

We have a total of 200 hours of work available to be scheduled. If we can schedule all 200 hours, we'll be at 100% Schedule Efficiency. However, last week we only scheduled 112 of those available hours. Therefore, our Schedule Efficiency was 112 hours scheduled ÷ 200 available hours x 100 or 56%.

In this example, we only schedule a little more than half of the available hours for the week! Too often this is the case. If we track our production hours we will know exactly how many hours we can produce in a week. Once we have that number, take out some time for upsells, tow ins, carryover, etc. and arrive at a number of hours you want to schedule. Get your Schedule Efficiency to 100% and watch the shop be constantly busy!

Total Revenue

This KPI is likely the most common number owners and managers pay attention to. Many service advisors get paid off this number, and as such it becomes the KPI everyone wants to see. Some people look at this number and say "but that's not representative of the money I have left to pay salaries, or grow business, etc.". They are right, but at the end of the day, Total Revenue is the money that came into the business.

This number is made up of both parts sales, labor sales, and any other source of revenue (towing, accessories, or the gum-ball machine). In general, you can say that roughly 50% of Total Revenue is parts and the rest is labor. This is a general guideline for making guestimates from and doesn't always work out exactly this way.

What this number should be will depend on your shop size, how many technicians you employ, what your production is, and many other factors. You can get close to what you should expect to see by using this formula:

(# of Bays x 8 hours x # of days open x Hourly rate) x 2

Think of it like this. Your service capacity assumes you have 1 technician for each bay. Each technician is 100% productive in our scenario and we are open 5 days each week. Our hourly rate is $100 per hour. Doing this first part of the math in the parentheses we end up with $16,000 each week in labor sales. Since this represents roughly half of our Total Revenue we then multiply our answer by 2 to get $32,000.For a 4 bay shop, this is a reasonable weekly revenue target. If we want to be even more accurate, and we know our average shop productivity percent, we can take the math in the parentheses and multiply the answer our average production before doubling it to get our Total Revenue target. For instance, let's say our shop is only 80% productive. This means that 4 technicians, working 8 hours each day, 5 days every week and charging $100 per hour will actually only bring in $12,800 in labor, making our actual target $24,000 Total Revenue. You can now see what the 20% drop in productivity represents in terms of total revenue! That's $8,000 each week we don't collect, or $32,000 each month, and $384,000 each year. That could mean the difference between making it in business, and going out of business!

Key Point

The average 4 bay repair shop should be able to bring in a yearly revenue of $1,600,000. Yes, this potential is real, however it takes some work.

Calculate your average shop production and from that figure out what you want to see for a revenue target. I always set my production targets at 100% production so that everyone in the organization has to push to attain the target. If you know your production is at 80%, then set the target using 90% production.

Key Point

I always set my production targets at 100% production so that everyone in the organization has to push to attain the target.

Once you have a Total Revenue target, put it in writing for each of your service counter employees and let them know where they stand each week. Before long you'll begin to hit those targets and it will be time to move them upward.

Gross Profit % per Job

If you want to increase your overall gross profit, focus on Gross Profit % per job. This is the single best way to grow the overall number consistently and without leaving to chance. The old adage of "take care of the pennies and the dollars will take care of themselves" is what this is all about. If we keep a consistent eye on the gross profit percent of each individual job, then the overall Gross Profit will take care of itself. Even if you want to focus on growing gross profit rather than revenue, or you happen to pay your people based on Gross Profit, watching this KPI on each job will get you where you want to go.

Gross Profit % per Job is calculated as Gross Profit (revenue minus direct expenses) compared to overall revenue. In other words, what percent of the total revenue in this job is the gross profit? The good news is that you won't have to calculate this number. Your Service Management System will have the calculation built in. Your service counter staff will have to check the number at the time each estimate is built though!

Something to Consider

Productivity of your technicians greatly affects a
shop's ability to bring in revenue.

What should the number be? It will depend on the job is the poor answer. Certain jobs, such as mount and balance tires, will have a lower GP% than a job such as an alignment. Your parts matrix will affect the GP% of each job as will the technician assigned to the job (higher paid technicians will reduce the GP%). This makes it so that there is no cut and dry answer to the question of "what should it be". In general I ask lesser performing shops to ensure each job has at least a 50% GP%. I can see some rolling their eyes out there, thinking 'good grief, you'll go out of business!'. Maybe, but if someone isn't used to looking at this number and it's currently 45% I don't want to ask for 65% as it seems too much of a stretch for many and may even affect the customer's perception of the shop.

If you are already around that 50% mark, then move the target up to 60%. You can go as high as 65% on many jobs without things getting so expensive that you are no longer competitive. Once this number begins to get watched, the next question is often 'how do I increase it?'. Good question. With the number of variables making it up, and your hands often tied by the parts pricing, the easiest thing to do is make sure your parts matrix is up-to-date and then pay attention to which technician the job is assigned to. If there is no choice as to who is going to do the work and you have a highly paid technician pulling down the GP% on a particular job, the next solution is to bump the labor times up on the job. Many SMS's have the ability to automatically apply a bump to labor times or labor dollars to account for this. See if yours does and set it somewhere around 15 to 20 percent.

For shop managers and owners who really want to grow their gross profit, the GP% per Job metric is a great way to do it. The calculation is done by the SMS and, in most cases, the only thing a service advisor has to do is check the number before finalizing the job estimate and calling the customer. Some systems even have the ability to set a notification if the GP% is below a certain threshold on any given job. If yours has this ability, set the notification threshold at a minimum of 60 or 65 percent depending on your preference and circumstances.

Use the Gross Profit % per Job performance indicator to make your business more profitable and make everyone more money.

Key Point

The old adage of "take care of the pennies and the dollars will take care of themselves" is what keeping an eye on GP% per Job is all about!

Net Profit %

Now here is a sometimes controversial KPI! Net Profit, or Net Profit as % of Sales is just what we said it was in the Financial Management Chapter 8 – what you get to keep. Looking at number is easy as basic accounting principles and definitions apply and most any accounting system will give you an accurate number as long as your accountant set it up properly. When looking at your Net Profit as a % of Sales, what should the number be? Different people will tell you different things of course. The best answer is: as high as it can possibly be! No kidding genius...

The reality is that most independent shops will hover somewhere around 10% if they are doing well. Dealership service departments don't generally worry about this number because they are part of a larger entity and they don't get to take the money home with them if they could. I've heard of, but have never seen myself, independent repair shops with a Net Profit Percent of Sales of 20%. If you can accomplish this in your shop, please give me a call!

I suggest shops set a target of 10% and pay close attention to their Gross Profit % per Job, overall shop Productivity %, and their Effective Labor Rate. As an owner, or manager, you'll have to get these numbers as high as possible and then keep a close eye on facility and salary expense. This is where the art of managing comes it. It can be easy to drive Net Profit by making cuts in expenses somewhere, but you have to balance the effect it will have on your customer satisfaction, ability to bring customers to the shop, and employee retention.

Focus on some of the other KPI's before worrying too much about Net Profit %....at least until you get a good feel for the other indicators.

RO's per Service Advisor

This may sound like a strange KPI to put in a list like this, and maybe it is, but I think it is important in terms of management. You will often hear service counter staff complain of being too busy. How can we ever quantify what it is to be too busy? We all feel busy with different levels of work and so as a manager just how do you make the determination that more staff is needed because everyone is so busy? I use the RO's per Service Advisor metric.

In the dealership world, due to much specialization and the many support systems in place, the guidelines state that each Service Advisor should be able to open, communicate, estimate, and close 18 to 20 repair orders each day. This is almost impossible in the independent repair shop world though. I recommend for most, non-dealership, repair shops that service counter staff should be able to handle 10 to 12 repair orders each day.

Something to Consider

When you think you might need to hire more non-production personnel, look into how many repair orders each advisor is handling already. This number will tell you if you're ready to hire.

If a Service Advisor is complaining of being too busy to make follow up phone calls, talk about your customer referral program to new customers, or is slacking on other responsibilities and they are handling 7 RO's each day, you need to make some observations as to how they are going about their work. If you discover they are averaging 15 repair orders each day then maybe they have a complaint.

Key Point

In a good independent repair shop, each service advisor should be able to write, keep track of, and invoice at least 10 repair orders each day. In a dealership this number is closer to 20.

Each shop is different, responsibilities of individuals may vary, and how many other support staff you have all will contribute to how many actual repair orders can be handled in a day. If you have no receptionist, and the service counter staff cash each customer out, answer every phone call, dispatch work to the shop, call for parts, and handle the rental cars, it's very possible that 10 repair orders each day is all that can be effectively done. If you are a shop with some additional support staff, then the 10 to 12 RO's each day per advisor might go up to 15 per day.

In any case, pay attention to how many RO's each person writes each day when determining the need for additional staff or workflow improvements at the counter and throughout the shop.

Choosing Which KPI to Watch

Each KPI covered so far is important to some aspect of the business, or in some cases, the entire business. There are other KPI's the industry has developed that you will hear talked about and espoused as the ones to really pay attention to. For me, the important part is that you are watching something. Completely ignoring the numbers and running the business by feel won't get you where you want to go. Most shop owners and managers discover that they were wrong about part of the business when they start to watch the numbers. Choose any of the KPI's in this chapter and begin to track it. If I had to choose for you, I'd pick Productivity % to get you started. The interesting thing about tracking any of these numbers is that once you do, you will begin to get an intuitive feel for what effects the numbers. This feel for the numbers helps you to understand what process changes need to be made, or improvements need to be implemented.

Remember not to solely relay on your service management system to give you the numbers related to these performance indicators. As good as these systems are, they have limitations in the way the data is collected and sometimes calculated. Understand what it is you want to track, and why. Begin tracking the number with paper and pencil to so that you establish a better understanding of the calculation and what affects the number. Once you have this understanding, then you can take numbers from the management system if you feel the data is accurately collected and/or calculated.

- **Key Performance Indicators are a critical piece to operating a successful business.**
- **Technician Productivity relates directly to what you sell – time.**
- **Gross Profit % per Job is a great way to keep an eye on, and grow Gross Profit one job at a time.**
- **KPI's can help you decide if you need to hire more personnel or make a capital investment in the business.**
- **Once you begin to track KPI's you will no longer be managing by "feel" but by what is real.**
- **When first beginning to track a Key Performance Indicator that is new to you, collect the data and make the calculation with paper and pencil to gain a better understanding of it.**
- **Use the KPI calculator on the Repair Shop Rescue app to quickly calculate your performance.**

Chapter 10: The Best Marketing

In This Chapter

- **Maximizing your marketing dollars.**
- **Only paying for marketing that works.**
- **Proven marketing practices.**

Marketing is something that every shop owner and manager knows they need. Let's face it though. Very few owners or managers are marketing experts. Of course, it's really hard for any of us to say, "I don't know" and so we go through our business lives acting like we know how to market. This is like me saying I'm a physicist. I'm not. Just because I can recite Newton's Second Law of Thermal Dynamics doesn't mean I should be building rockets. Just because we've all seen some marketing and advertising doesn't mean we should be designing and delivering marketing for our shops...yet we do.

Something to Consider

Unless you have formal education in marketing, it's usually best to hire a professional, or stick with those marketing activities that don't require content creation or market strategy.

When we don't know, it also makes it really easy for a good salesperson to get us to purchase marketing that looks like it will work. A direct mail salesperson will tell us all about guarantees that our flyer will land in 20,000 households and that we can expect a 5% return. We do the math and think "Wow, a thousand new customers. That's awesome!" never realizing that a 1% is the industry average and very few shops will even see that much.

In this chapter, I'll give away my marketing secrets. As with most everything else in the automotive repair industry, I believe in keeping things simple and staying with the things that work. Everything I'm putting down here has been proven to work in virtually every market, maximizes your marketing money spent, and costs next to nothing or will only cost you if it does work.

It All Begins with Quality

You will have nothing if you don't have quality. I believe this is so important that I'm writing about it again here. Yes, you've read about it in Managing the Shop, but in case you missed something here it is again. Without quality workmanship and Fixed Right the First Time (remember Chapter 1) you will only spend marketing money to try and get new, unsuspecting customers through the door. Eventually your reputation will precede you and it will be only those broken down on the highway as they pass through on vacation and get "lucky" enough to be towed to your shop that you will be able to attract. Before anything else in this book matters, you *must* have quality. No quality, no customers. No quality, wasted time dealing with distractions and thinking of how to grow car count.

Key Point

Without quality, you have nothing. No amount of money spent on marketing will overcome poor, or inconsistent quality workmanship. Always have a quality control process in place to ensure quality.

Your shop needs to have a quality control program implemented for *each and every vehicle* that leaves the shop. This means that every oil change, tire rotation, alignment, engine job, brake job, or dome light repair gets quality controlled. Quality never quits. Quality gets you more customers for free.

Your quality control program begins with your technician's taking responsibility for quality control, continues with a quality control inspection, and finishes with a signature of commitment. Again, here is what I recommend:

1. The technician who performed the work test drives the vehicle after he/she performs the required service.

2. A second set of eyes (a "quality control buddy", shop foreman, etc.) reviews the work done, asks questions, and makes sure there are no obvious cleanliness issues.

3. For bigger jobs, a second test drive is conducted by a Quality Control Manager, Shop Foreman, or other dedicated person.

4. Once the vehicle has been inspected twice, the technician who performed the work, Quality Control Manager (if one is designated) and Service Advisor sign off that a quality control process has been completed.

You're probably thinking that this is time consuming, and way too much for just an oil change. Think about how time consuming doing an engine replacement for free will be! The reality is that the process goes much faster over time. The oil change QC can be just a visual inspection by the performing technician, very quick test drive, and a second visual inspection (oil cap, oil on dipstick, sticker in window, no oil underneath the vehicle) by the same technician, and then the signature.

Something to Consider

Implement a quality control process and let it run for a month. Meet with everyone involved after that first month and make improvements to the system for efficiency and consistency of the process.

The point to having a quality control process is not to slow production down, but to create an environment where customers begin to trust your work to the point that they don't think of going anywhere else and want to talk about you. Quality work creates peace of mind for the customer, easier work days for you (no disgruntled customers, high production, fewer problems to deal with), and a base from which to market from.

Key Point

Always have at least one person sign off that the Quality Control Process has been completed. This will build accountability in employees and impress your customers

---

Let me quickly mention the signature aspect of this process. There are a number of ways shops will have those responsible for QC sign off on the process. It can be a technician business card with a "proudly quality controlled by" signature line on it, a mirror hang tag with the same design, or just a signature line added to the repair order. No matter how you collect the signature, the reason to do so is not only to show the customer that the shop, and individual care about the work performed, but to create accountability to the process with everyone. Just as the customer signature creates a level of buy in with the repair process, the QC signature creates buy in with consistent quality.

Customer Referral Program

Once you've established quality, the next thing that needs to be done is to make it easy for customers to talk about you. Not only should it be easy for them to talk about you, but you may even want to incentivize them to talk about you. As was mentioned in a previous chapter, customers are constantly searching for a repair shop that they can rely on. When they find one that can be trusted to consistently provide quality work, a great service experience, and a fair price they will tell anyone who asks, and many who don't ask!

Something to Consider

A customer referral program should be at the core of your marketing program. They are inexpensive to implement and are 100% effective.

A customer referral program is the best marketing I can imagine. There are so many positive aspects to implementing and maintaining one I don't know where to start. Imagine a marketing campaign that you only pay for if it brings you a customer. How much would you be willing to pay for such a program? If you have an ARO of $325 would you be willing to pay 25, 50, or 75 dollars to get a new customer and only have

---

Something to Consider

When you develop a Customer Referral program put it in writing. This helps educate new hires, provides content copy for advertising, and is a basis for improvement at time goes on.

---

to pay that fee once? I can't imagine a business person in any industry who wouldn't say yes to that deal!

Not only is customer referral a no-brainer from a financial perspective its effectiveness cannot be beat. A referral from a friend, family member, or even acquaintance comes with a built-in level of trust. That level of trust allows you to get off to an even better start with the new customer. It also means that your advertising is likely to work (of course, you won't pay for it unless it does). When someone recommends a product or service to you, you are far more likely to purchase that product or service, and be happy with it.

One more thing, what if this piece of advertising magic has a customer retention piece that will keep your existing customers from going anywhere? Sound too good to be true? It's not!

Here's what your program should be:

1. A customer takes one of your business cards and writes their name on the back of the card.

2. This customer then hands off the business card to someone they want to refer to your repair shop.

3. When that new customer arrives with the business card, you note the name written on the back of the card and that customer receives a $50 credit to their account.

4. The new customer then is informed of the referral program and has the opportunity to do the same if they are happy with the level of service you provide.

The program is simple and easy both to implement and maintain. Begin by having business cards printed with a line on the front, or back, where a customer (or service advisor), can write their name on it. Next, have a counter display (counter top mat, sticker, or framed display) created so make your waiting room customers want to ask about how they earn free service and repair. Then, decide how much money you want to reward the referring customer with.

When it comes to reward, there was a reason I asked how much you would pay for such a program earlier. Paying a customer $50 in return for an ARO of $325 is a good deal – for both of you. You pay $50 once for an average of 2 RO's per year of $325. In other words, you paid $50 in return for $600 in revenue. For some shop owners, this is too much money to "give a customer". I disagree, but if you still feel that way then use $25. This is still enough money that it will accumulate fast enough in the customer's account for them to recognize the very real benefit of the program and keep them coming back to you, and only you, for service and repair.

Key Point

You want to find that one individual who recognizes the value referring other customers has to them and turn them loose to give out as many referral cards as they can.

The ultimate goal is to find that one individual who recognizes the value of the program and begins passing our referral after referral. They may never have to pay for vehicle repair again, and imagine the number of customers this person will send you. All with a program that you only pay for if the new customer shows up.

The initial investment that must be made is in the business cards, posters, counter displays and other advertising. Once the program is implemented you just need to keep it present on your website, in your print advertising, and ensure your employees are all talking about it. You can even use it as an employee referral program with the money to be put toward tool or parts purchases.

One last suggestion for using the program, is to have whomever is cashing out your customers, take a card, write the customer's name on the card, and staple it to the invoice with a reminder to use the program. After a while it will become common practice and a majority of your customers will know of, and use, the program. That is marketing money well spent.

Newsletters and Email Campaigns

When it comes to advertising, any advertising you do is likely to enter a sea of other automotive marketing bombarding customers every day. Therefore, I don't generally ask my clients to do any direct mail, radio, or television advertising. Not only are these expensive, but they are minimally effective. In my opinion, the best thing you can do is create some direct-to-your-customer mail and email pieces that connect your repair shop with your customer. These pieces should not be sent so often that they become commonplace, yet often enough to be a reminder. They also must stand out.

Newsletters are a great way of connecting to customers if they are done well. A good newsletter can be time consuming and is not the most inexpensive form of advertising, but it can be very effective. The key to making a newsletter effective is the timing and content of the piece. Receiving a newsletter too often makes it difficult for you to find content and creates some complacency with customers. A newsletter that only talks about you and how awesome you are becomes old news and not something anyone looks forward to seeing.

When designing a newsletter, it must contain information on local events and happenings, causes your shop or employees support, current promotions, business partner promotions, and some sort of fun – games, contests, funny stories, etc. If you can afford it, a great impression can be made when it's all done in color. It doesn't have to be very long to be effective.

It just needs to be long enough to include the above content with photos. Some shops have even subsidized the cost of producing the newsletter by selling advertising in it to local businesses. They can allow business partners less expensive advertising because you are not trying to make a business out of the newsletter, but only pay for the cost of content development and printing.

In terms of content development, you may be thinking that you are no content expert, and you may be correct. Often shops will outsource the creation and mailing of newsletters and only must provide shop related content to the publisher. This pushes costs higher than they would be if you had someone in-house to do it, but it reduces some stress as well and can ensure consistent quality in content.

Key Point

Email marketing can be challenging. There is still a good return on it, however the filters get better and better as time goes on and fewer and fewer customers see the emails now.

If a newsletter is too much for you to take on right now, then start with an email campaign. I'm not convinced that email marketing is what it used to be, but it is still a way to stay connected to customers. A single page, color, email that is well designed and includes an opt-in for the customer can be as effective as a newsletter and more cost effective in many cases.

The challenge with email is that email filters have gotten so good now that unless you have the email designed by a professional who knows how to work around many of the filters put in place…and can continually do so, you may be wasting a lot of time on email that gets deleted.

Just like with the newsletter, email marketing must be timed so that customers do not receive too much of it, but enough to stay connected. In terms of general guidelines, sending six newsletters or email per year with interesting content is enough to stay connected. With email, you'll probably be sending service reminders and recommendations as well, so email contact becomes monthly sometimes. Another reason to send six newsletters via regular post, rather than use email.

Whether you create a newsletter or choose to rely on email to connect your customers to the shop in between service visits, make sure you create a piece that ties your shop to the community, your customers, and local events. Doing so lets your customers know that you're more than just about selling service and parts and will go a long way in building the all-important trust.

Seasonal Specials

No matter what advertising you engage in, it needs to be effective. To make it effective, it must connect to the customer in such a way that they recognize the need for whatever it is you're advertising. Today, there are very few aspects of the automobile that customers connect to. Oil changes are still recognized as being needed, but not as much as they once were, tires still wear out and create a safety, handling or inspection challenge that customers have an awareness of, and brakes still must stop the car. I recommend leveraging those things that customers have an awareness of in your seasonal advertising campaigns.

I like seasonal advertising campaigns a lot because not only can they connect to a customer based on something the customer recognizes a need for, but they can also be created such that they are easy to reuse each year. This minimizes the amount of work and creates consistency and habit with both employees and customers. It also maximizes any investment you make in printing, equipment purchases, or training.

Seasonal advertising is easier in some parts of the country (or world) than it is in others. In areas that observe four seasons, customers very often have definite needs as each season changes. Tire change over, air conditioning, alignments, and winter check-ups make great seasonal specials. Combine these with a number of other incentives like your referral program, a discounted oil change or free wiper blades, and suddenly you have an effective campaign to be used each season.

Let's look at some examples of specials you could use:

Spring Alignment Special

Spring is a time of renewal, roads are filled with potholes, and it's been a long winter in some places. Capitalize on this renewal idea and let customers know you can "set their vehicle right again". Your spring special should include a free alignment check, free tire rotation, and a discounted oil change. You might also include a battery inspection, cabin air filter promotion, or wiper blades.

Your promotional material should mention how often an automobile should have an alignment, what an out-of-alignment vehicle looks like, and what is done during the alignment.

Summer Air Conditioning Special

This promotion works very well as customers have a strong awareness of wanting their air condition to work! There are a couple of different ways to run this special as well. With either of the options below, combine it with a discount oil change, battery inspection, tire rotation, and courtesy inspection.

You could just promote a Free A/C Inspection that includes a vent temperature reading, visual inspection and static pressure reading (not necessary, but it's just one more piece of data to sell with). If something is found during the inspection you then would upsell a recover/recharge with dye and further inspection.

Some shops will just advertise the recharge and inspection. This can work, however you'll catch more business with the free inspection as it captures the attention of even those customers that just love 'free' and don't necessarily think they have a problem. Remember, even if it is free, it allows you to get the car into the bay, up in the air, and eyes on it.

Fall "Prepare for Winter" Special

In the parts of the world where winter is imminent, fall is a time for preparation. Customers are in a preparation mindset and are tuned into the fact they need tires changed, batteries checked, coolant systems serviced, etc. Capitalize on the necessity of being safe driving in some of the world's worse weather with a Fall Preparation special. As with the other specials combine it with discounted air filters, coolant services, free inspections, and wiper blade promotions.

An important note about seasonal specials, and advertising in general. Your mission with advertising is to get the vehicle into the shop, in the air, with the wheels off. In order to do this, the customer must recognize a need to bring it to you. Your seasonal specials play on these recognized needs so that the customer brings the vehicle to you and gives you permission to inspect the vehicle. Use local conditions, seasonal changes, and knowledge of your specific market to find those things that are really important to your customers. From that, create marketing or advertising that visually shows the customer you know what it's like to live here and have to prepare for summer heat, winter ice, spring mud, or fall rain.

Key Point

Don't take your website for granted. It's easy to let it be the last thing to pay attention to, but changing content, specials, updating employee bios, etc. keeps it fresh and at the top of search results.

Your Website

One of the more important, and sometimes most frustrating, methods of marketing your automotive repair shop will use is your website. We have become so used to websites now that many owners and managers feel like they have them just because you're not in business unless you do have one. The fact that creating a website, and then maintaining it, can be expensive and frustrating contributes to many businesses just letting the site sit out there in virtual space. This is a mistake you should not make.

Most of your customers today will find you through word of mouth, or online searches. This makes your website more than just a form of marketing, but an integral tool in the growth of your business. You want your website to not only attract a customer who is searching for services, but to allow them to understand who you are, how you do business, engage with your products and services, and see how others feel about doing business with you.

Even more than all of this (as if that wasn't enough) you also want your website to position your shop, and employees, as the experts. In a world where answers are mere finger taps away, there is a lot of information out there as to what you need, why, and how much to pay. You want to be the primary source of information on auto repair and maintenance for your customers so that you spend less time explaining why something they saw, or read, was wrong, and why you do things you do the way you do them.

Something to Consider

Use your website to position your shop as the experts in automotive service. Customers have questions and will search the internet for answers. Be the one they go to for their service and maintenance questions.

A well-designed website helps to create transparency in the auto repair process, allows customers to see and understand who you are as an organization, and lets them engage you in business. It must be dynamic enough, changing often enough, that search engines place you near the top of the search results. The technologies and methodologies for making sure you end up on top of the search results list is ever changing, and so what worked to keep you up there yesterday may not work tomorrow. Your website needs the constant attention of a professional to truly work for you.

What should your website include? Here is my list:

Your Company Philosophy or Mission

There is much talk today about establishing a niche in the auto repair industry. Really, what a niche boils down to, is a specific way of doing business with a specific market. If you specialize in foreign auto repair, performance modifications, or have specialized service equipment for a certain market segment, your website should say so. It should also convey the fact that you believe in honest, transparent auto repair.

Biographies of Your Employees

These bios don't need to be long, but they should be kept up to date in terms of how long these folks have been with you, the kind of experience and training they have, and what their personal interests and passions are. Short biographies of your employees, along with photos, make your organization human. It connects the customer with your people both before and after they meet your organization. Many times customers will tell me they choose to do business with a certain shop because they know an employee shares a passion or philosophy.

This could be through church, volunteer efforts, or membership to certain organizations.

Location with Map and Directions

Don't assume your customers, and potential customers, know where to find you or how to give directions to a referral. Make it easy to find you via your website.

Ability to Schedule Appointments

This is a tough one as I write this. There are some companies trying to work out the technology to connect your website scheduling app to the service management system, but unless you are a dealership you'll be unlikely to make this a seamless process for another few years. In the meantime, you'll have to put up with some short term pain in order to win over some customers. There are many widgets that can capture when a customer wants to visit and collect their information but very few, if any, that can tell the customer when you have availability in your schedule. The pain is that the customer will choose when to arrive and you will have to make accommodations to fit them in…whether you like it or not. As more and more customers are choosing to do business over their smartphone these days, appointment scheduling via website is more and more important.

FAQ Section

This is where you can position yourself as the expert. Including an FAQ section, or even a video FAQ section on your website, can not only help create some transparency in the repair process but can give customers a trusted source of information. Including things like:

- What oil should I use?

- What's it mean when my Check Engine Light comes on?

- How often should I have my vehicle aligned?

- Should I purchase premium brake pads, or the cheap ones?

- My car shakes while driving. What could the problem be?

- Why do shops have such a high hourly labor rate?

Answering these questions, and more, can get customers to begin seeing you as someone who is there to help them rather than just take advantage of the fact they need their car worked on. Being able to answer these questions in a quick one-minute video blog can be even more effective because now it personalizes things for the customer.

There are many other things your website should have: contact information, common services, towing services, emergency roadside assistance programs, warranty information links, etc. All those things you get questions about from your customers should appear somewhere on your website.

Last, but not least…make sure your website is mobile friendly. It should go without saying, however there so many non-mobile friendly websites out there that its worth reminding everyone!

When To Engage Marketing

The last thing that I'll say about cost effective marketing that really works is that you can never stop. A big mistake many managers and owners make is seeing the shop getting busier, and busier, and then discontinuing the marketing. This begins a pendulum ride. Once you stop marketing, it takes a while for things to catch up and begin to slow down. Eventually slower days arrive and we start to think we need to begin marketing again. Yet, as it took time for things to slow down, it takes time for marketing to bring in business. The time to market is when you are busy.

Your marketing should be consistent. No matter what marketing media you engage in, it must be consistent. If the cost is so high that you cannot afford to keep going with the print ad, radio ad, or newspaper print ad, don't get into it. Potential customers not only need to see that you are a business, but must see that you are a business that can help them, when they need help. You have no idea when they might need help, thus you must always be present in the market.

The ideas presented in this chapter are easy to implement, inexpensive to continue, and will bring you customers. Encourage your employees to talk about your quality control program, engage customers in the customer referral program, and promote seasonal specials. Making these programs a part of everyday business will keep you from being inconsistent with your core marketing.

For more talk about marketing for the real world, visit the training videos on the Repair Shop Rescue app. If you're thinking of improving your marketing, or starting a marketing campaign, these videos support the ideas presented here, and bring to light other aspects to consider, along with more ideas for effective marketing.

Always Remember

- Everything begins with quality work. Quality is your marketing base.
- Your customers are your best source of advertising. Make it easy for them to talk about you – and reward them for it.
- A well-designed newsletter can be an effective marketing tool.
- Keep your website up-to-date. Engage a professional to conduct SEO and social media management for you.
- Position yourself, and your employees to be the expert. Customers will use the internet for answers – be the one they know they can get honest answers from.
- Make yourself present in the community. Encourage employees to join volunteer efforts or hobby groups and let them wear their logo wear to events.
- Never stop marketing. When you need the business, it's too late to begin marketing.

Thought Starters

The following pages contain exercises intended to help guide
you with the changes you'd like to make in the operation of
your repair shop. These exercises focus on Customers, Service Writers, the Customer Experience, Technicians, and
Shop Management. Use them to start thinking about how and
why you might make positive changes in your service operation.

Thought Starter 1: Customers

List four (4) places where you are currently a customer:

1. _____
   _____

2. _____
   _____

3. _____
   _____

4. _____
   _____

Recall a single incident where you were the disgruntled customer.

1. Why were you unhappy?

   _____
   _____

_____

_____

2. What was done to remedy the situation?

_____

_____

_____

_____

3. How do you think the situation could have been handled better?

_____

_____

_____

_____

Based on the 'Types of Customers' information:

1. What type of customer are you?

_____

_____

2. What type of customer is your husband/wife/significant other?

_____

_____

Think of the last time you dealt with an upset customer at the service desk.

1. How could things have been handled better?

_____

_____

_____

_____

_____

_____

_____

2. Could the situation have been avoided?

_____

_____

_____

_____

_____

_____

_____

3. Is there a process that could be implemented to avoid a similar situation in the future? If so, what?

_____

_____

_____

_____

_____

_____

_____

_____

_____

_____

_____

_____

_____

Thought Starter 2: The Customer Service Experience

Scheduling

1. Do you have any challenges with your scheduling system as it is currently configured? If so, what are they specifically?

   _____
   _____
   _____
   _____
   _____
   _____
   _____
   _____

2. What would you like to see improved about your current scheduling processes?

   _____
   _____
   _____
   _____
   _____
   _____
   _____
   _____

3. Name one thing that you could implement in the next 30 days that would improve the scheduling process at your repair shop.

_____

_____

_____

_____

_____

_____

_____

_____

Fixed Right First Time

1. What is one thing that could be implemented in your repair shop over the next 30 days that would improve *Fixed Right First Time* for your customers?

_____

_____

_____

_____

_____

_____

_____

_____

_____

Thought Starter 3: Service Writers

Service Writer Incentives

How are your service writers currently paid?

_____

_____

_____

_____

_____

_____

_____

In an ideal environment how would like to pay
your service writers?

_____

_____

_____

_____

_____

_____

_____

List **four** things you might base incentives for
your service writers on. Are they measurable?
Controllable?

1._____

_____

2._____

_____

3._____

_____

4._____

_____

Pick one of the above incentives that you listed and write down a rough formula for how you might structure a pay plan.

_____

_____

_____

_____

_____

_____

_____

What might the pitfalls be?

1._____

_____

2._____
_____

3._____
_____

4._____
_____

Will this incentive help drive customer satisfaction? How?

_____
_____
_____
_____
_____
_____
_____

Comebacks

What is one process you can implement in the next 30 days that would serve to reduce comebacks?

_____
_____

_____

_____

_____

_____

_____

_____

What would you need to implement this process?

Cost:

_____

_____

_____

Personnel:

_____

_____

_____

Materials:

_____

_____

_____

Thought Starter 4: Technicians

Vocational School Relationships

Do you currently have a relationship with your
local vocational school?   YES   NO

Who are your local vocational schools?

_____
_____
_____
_____
_____
_____
_____

Do you currently have a technician that you
think might make a good mentor?

_____
_____
_____
_____
_____
_____
_____

Interviewing

What does your ideal interview process look like?

_____
_____
_____
_____
_____
_____
_____

In addition to the questions suggested in the text, list six questions you would ask a potential technician:

1._____
_____

2._____
_____

3._____
_____

4._____

_____

5._____

_____

6._____

_____

Technician Pay Plans

How do you currently pay your technicians?

Flat Rate　　　　**Hourly**　　　　**Other**

If you were to combine flat rate and hourly pay plans, what do you believe a good plan might look like?

_____
_____
_____
_____
_____
_____
_____

Thought Starter 5: Shop Management

Technical Training

Do you currently send your technicians to technical training?   YES   NO

In what areas do you feel your technicians need to improve?

_____
_____
_____
_____
_____
_____

Does your current training provider present curriculum in these areas?

            YES   NO   I DON'T KNOW

If not, have you asked them for it?

_____

_____

_____

_____

_____

_____

_____

_____

Hours of Operation

What are your current hours of operation?

_____

_____

_____

_____

_____

_____

_____

Have/would you consider being open Saturdays?

_____

_____

_____

Based on the alternative work schedule description. how many technicians would you need to add to create an alternative work schedule?

_____
_____
_____
_____
_____
_____
_____

If you were to increase your operating hours by 20%, how much would this add to your bottom line? (You can also think of this as how much is your single day revenue average?)

_____
_____
_____
_____
_____
_____
_____
_____
_____
_____
_____
_____

Labor Rate

Current Labor Rate:

_____

_____

_____

Ideal Labor Rate:

_____

_____

_____

Describe your ideal customer:

_____

_____

_____

_____

_____

_____

_____

_____

_____

Thought Starter 6: Best Practices

Of the Best Practices you've read about, which practices do you think would benefit your repair shop the most?

_____

_____

_____

_____

_____

_____

_____

Of the practices listed previously, which could you implement in the next 30 days?

_____

_____

_____

_____

_____

_____

_____

What would you need to implement these practices?

Practice 1:

_____

_____

Budget:

_____

_____

Personnel:

_____

_____

Tools:

_____

_____

Materials:

_____

_____

Practice 2:

_____

_____

Budget:

_____

_____

Personnel:

_____

_____

Tools:

_____

_____

Materials:

_____

_____

Practice 3:

_____

_____

Budget:

_____

_____

Personnel:

_____

_____

Tools:

_____

_____

Materials:

_____

_____

Practice 4:

_____

_____

Budget:

_____

_____

Personnel:

_____

_____

Tools:

_____

_____

Materials:

_____

_____

_____

Appendix

Appendix A: Automotive Service Best Practices

The following is a reference list of automotive service industry best practices. The list is ever evolving, so feel free to add your own best practices!

- Utilize alternate work schedules to be open during the most convenient work hours for your customers.
- Create incentivized pay plans for your technicians and service writers in order to encourage them to grow your business.
- Create giveaway programs for your employees to encourage certain behaviors. Pull boards, pull-tab game cards, etc. can be used to encourage technicians and service writers to sell certain promotions, or increase labor hours sold.
- Create displays utilizing new and old parts to demonstrate to customers the need for replacement.
- Offer a shuttle service.
- Encourage technicians to keep the shop clean, neat, and organized.
- Install windows between the waiting area and the work bays so that customers can see their vehicle being serviced.
- Keep the customer waiting area clean, neat, and pleasant.

- Provide training to your technicians and your service writers. Quality training can be found in areas of diagnostics, customer handling, and "soft skills".

- Keep up the appearance of your repair shop. New repair shops are being built with tile floors, drop ceilings, and a uniform look. If you want to compete in the market you must keep up your appearances!

- Offer your customers some form of warranty. Not only does it make them feel more secure about spending money, it sends a message to your employees that you care about the quality of work being done in the shop. A warranty expresses confidence in the work being delivered.

- Pay attention to the details. Customers are very anxious about having their vehicle serviced. The smallest things like quality coffee, plants in the waiting area, or comfortable seating can make them feel more at ease.

- Create a customer loyalty program. There are many ways to do this, but reward your customers for returning to your shop.

- Utilize an email marketing campaign that rewards customers for loyalty, provides customer satisfaction follow up, and reminds them of upcoming appointments.

- Hold quarterly or yearly open houses on weekends.

- Give away a service once or twice a year. Imagine the customer's surprise to know they just "won" a free service!

- Work with local vocational schools. Sit on an advisory committee, give presentations to the students on the automotive industry, or donate your time to the program. It will help you gain a positive reputation and you will find some quality employees through your relationship with the school.

- Keep all shop equipment in good repair.

- Provide your customers with seasonal specials. Coolant flushes and battery checks, winter tire specials, air conditioning specials will help drive traffic to your business. Incentivize employees to upsell these specials.

- Create a children's play area in your waiting room.

- Create a customer satisfaction follow up program. Randomly follow up on your customer's service experience via the phone. This shows your customers that you are concerned about the quality of service they received from your repair shop.

- Create an employee recognition program to reinforce employee loyalty.

Appendix B: Alternative Work Schedule Example

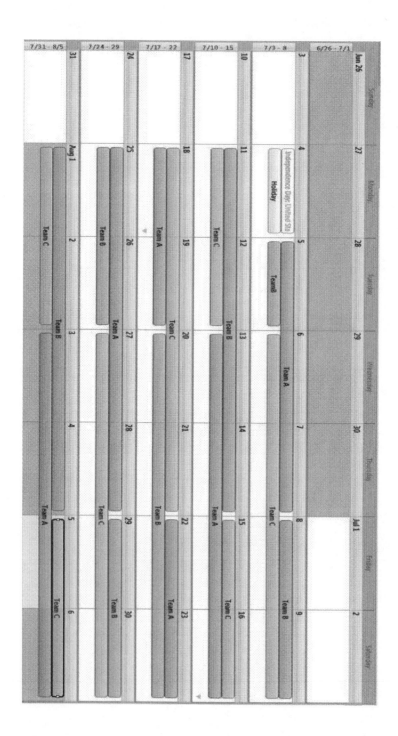

Appendix C: Customer Problem Analysis Sheet

Customer Problem Analysis Sheet

Customer: _____   Model/Year: _____

VIN: _____   Mileage: _____

Problem
Description: _____
_____
_____

Dates
Problem
Occurred: _____

Problem
Happens:
☐ Constantly   ☐ Occasionally: _____times per _____ day/month

☐ Once only   ☐ Other _____

☐ Daytime   ☐ Nighttime

Weather:
☐ Rainy   ☐ Sunny   ☐ Snowy

☐ Hot   ☐ Warm   ☐ Cool   ☐ Cold

☐ Temperature _____ F C

Location:
☐ Highway   ☐ City   ☐ Suburbs   ☐ Uphill

☐ Downhill   ☐ Idling   ☐ Turning: R / L

Engine
Temperature:
☐ Cold   ☐ Warm   ☐ Normal Operating Temp.

Other:
☐ Starting   ☐ Just after start: _____mins   ☐ Idling

☐ Driving   ☐ Speed: _____   ☐ Acceleration   ☐ Deceleration

Appendix D: Balance Sheet Example

John's Advanced Auto Service

Balance Sheet

	2010	2011		2010	2011
ASSETS			*LIABILITIES AND STOCKHOLDERS' EQUITY*		
			Current Liabilities		
Current Assets			Wages Payable	$0	$0
Cash	$23,597	$24,538	Accounts Payable	34,893	35,871
Marketable Securities	0	0	Taxes Payable	1,283	894
Accounts Receivable,			Other	35,981	42,198
Net of Uncollectible			Total Current		
Accounts	2000	150	Liabilities	$72,157	$78,963
Inventory	15000	12657	Long-Term Liabilities		
Other	0	0	Mortgage Payable	$98,327	$85,612
Prepaid Expenses	0	0	Bond Payable	0	0
Total Current Assets	$40,597	$37,345	Deferred Taxes	0	0
			Other	0	0
Fixed Assets			Total Long-Term		
Buildings and Equipment	$150,826	$134,792	Liabilities	$98,327	$85,612
Less Accumulated			Stockholders' Equity		
Depreciation	6297	2746	Common Stock, $X Par	$0	$0
Net Buildings and			Com. Stock-Excess		
Equipment	$144,529	$132,046	over par	0	0
Land	0	0	Preferred Stock, X%,		
Other	4675	7824	$X Par, X shares	0	0
Total Fixed Assets	$149,204	$139,870	Retained Earnings	26,808	21,324
			Total Stockholders'	$26,808	$21,324
Goodwill	0	358	Equity		
Other	7491	8326	TOTAL LIABILITIES		
			& STOCKHOLDERS'		
TOTAL ASSETS	$197,292	$185,899	EQUITY	$197,292	$185,899

Service Management Made Simple

Appendix E: Statement of Cash Flow Example

John's Advanced Auto Service

Statement of Cash Flows

For the Years Ending June 30,2010 and June 30,2011

Cash Flows from Operating Activities

Collections from Customers	$651,783
Payments to Suppliers	-243784
Payments to Employees	-190417
Reduction in Accounts Receivable	5691
Increase in Accounts Receivable	0
Increase in Accounts Payable	2537
Decrease in Accounts Payable	-2567
Increase in Inventory	-45891
Ammortization of Goodwill	0
Other	0
Net Cash from Operating Activities	$177,352

Cash Flows from Investing Activities

Purchase of New Equipment	-$55,786
Other	-53,596
Net Cash Used for Investing Activities	-$109,382

Cash Flows from Financing Activities

Borrowing from Creditors	$23,568
Issuance of Stock	0
Payment of Dividends	0
Other	0
Net Cash from Financing Activities	$23,568

NET INCREASE/(DECREASE) IN CASH	$91,538
CASH, BEGINNING OF YEAR	78923
CASH, END OF YEAR	$170,461

Service Management Made Simple

Appendix F: Income Statement Example

John's Advanced Auto Service

Statement of Income

For the Years Ending June 30,2010 and June 30,2011

		2010		2011
Revenues	$	862,578.00	$	901,892.00
Less Cost of Goods Sold	$	150,789.00	$	178,459.00
Gross Profit	$	711,789.00	$	723,433.00
Operating Expenses	$	56,721.00	$	43,581.00
Selling Expenses	$	22,457.00	$	21,897.00
Other	$	6,879.00	$	5,998.00
General Expenses	$	37,589.00	$	26,802.00
Administrative Expenses	$	44,789.00	$	49,012.00
Total Operating Expenses	$	111,714.00	$	147,290.00
Operating Income	$	600,075.00	$	576,143.00
Interest Expense	$	3,893.00	$	5,498.00
Income Before Taxes	$	596,182.00	$	570,645.00
Income Taxes	$	60,932.00	$	59,781.00
Net Income	$	535,250.00	$	510,864.00

Appendix G: Six Step Diagnostic Process

This diagnostic process can be applied to virtually any repair. It is most effective when used with electrical diagnostics, or engine control diagnostics, but can be adapted to fit any type of vehicle diagnosis.

As with all diagnostic processes, it is important not to skip steps!

Six Step Diagnostic Approach

1. **Verify the Concern**

2. **Determine Related Symptoms**

3. **Analyze Symptoms**

4. **Isolate the Concern**

5. **Repair the Concern**

6. **Verify Repair**

Appendix H: Technical Training Resources

The following is a list of training resources where a shop owner or manager can find technical training, soft-skill training, and management training. This is not intended to be a comprehensive list. Consult your industry associations for further training resources.

ShopPros

Toronto, ON Canada

www.shoppros.com

Repair Shop Rescue Coach

PO Box 836

Forestdale, MA 02644

877 488 5472

www.rsrcoach.com

Service Sales Academy

2635 E. Millbrook Rd

Raleigh, NC 27604

www.servicesalesacademy.com

CarQuest Technical Institute

2635 E. Millbrook Rd

Raleigh, NC 27604

www.carquest.com/proCTI

Automotive Service Association

P.O. Box 929

Bedford, Texas 76095

800 272 7467

www.asashop.org

Index

About the Author

Greg Marchand has over 34 years of unique experience in the automotive industry. Greg began his career as an independent shop owner before becoming a dealership technician, assistant service manager, college professor, manufacturer representative, and owner of AAT, Inc. Greg also leads the Service Sales Academy.

During a 12-year career with Toyota Motor Sales, USA Greg served as a Field Technical Specialist, Service Training Specialist, and Parts and Service Development Consultant. As a P&S Development Consultant for Toyota, Greg worked with dealership parts and service departments on a daily basis to increase service retention, customer satisfaction, and implement employee training programs.

As his career evolved within the industry Greg began designing and delivering knowledge rich, engaging automotive service and sales curriculum for instructor led and virtual instructor led training programs delivered throughout the U.S., Canada, and Europe. At one point he served as Special Advisor to the President of Kia Motors Adria Group where he oversaw all aspects of new vehicle distribution, sales, and service support throughout eight Central European countries. Greg is currently the Chief Operating Officer of ShopPros – a software company based in Canada that provides learning and business management products to the automotive industry.

Greg holds an undergraduate degree in Automotive Technology and an MBA in Organizational Sustainability. His spare time is spent fishing, skiing, and ice climbing.

Service Management Made Simple

Acknowledgments

I would like to thank the multitude of individuals and organizations that made this book possible. All the service managers, dealership principles, coworkers, independent repair shop owners, automotive consultants, and industry professionals that I've had the pleasure of meeting and working with over the years have had an influence on this book. Without these professionals, our industry would not be what it is today, and I would not have the ability to do what I do for a living. I continue to learn from managers, owners, and industry representatives daily and could never thank them enough.

A special thank you goes out to Jennifer Elder who advised and reviewed the Financial Management chapter, Peter Marchand who assisted with the cover design, Phil Cicio who continues to inspire me, and to my family for putting up with my work schedule.

DRIVEN TO SUCCEED

MASTERMIND GROUP

Building Freedom and Financial Security With The Business Of Your Dreams

Join a group of high-performing Automotive Shop Owners interested in learning and growing together to take their time back, increase financial security, manage employees, reduce stress, grow market penetration, and find freedom

MASTERMIND

Expect to be challenged to perform your best, to be held accountable by the group, to present to the group at least once each year, to share ideas, successes, and failures. When you put the work in, expect your shop to quickly grow into the organization of your dreams.

ShopPros
Accelerating success.

Save 10% when you pay annually

$2,495 Per Month
Billed Monthly

$2,245.50 Per Month
Billed Annually at $26,946

Weekly Meetings | Bi-Annual In Person Events | Gross Profit & Advisor Training Programs | BusinessPro Access for goal setting, revenue projection, financial planning & accountability | Employee Accountability Tools | Facebook Closed Group | Marketing & Car Count Insight | Increasing Profit & Goal Setting | Industry Trends and More

Made in the USA
Middletown, DE
04 September 2024

59713659R00183